- *Jonathan Kozol*
- *Dorothea Lange*
- *Lewis Lapham*
- *Frances Moore Lappé*
- *Perry Mann*
- *John Muir*
- *Ralph Nader*
- *Rosa Parks*
- *Paul Robeson*
- *Eleanor Roosevelt*
- *Frank Serpico*
- *Margaret Chase Smith*
- *Samantha Smith*
- *Elizabeth Cady Stanton*
- *Louis "Studs" Terkel*
- *Henry David Thoreau*
- *Sojourner Truth*
- *Mark Twain*
- *Ida B. Wells*
- *Walt Whitman*
- *Judy Wicks*
- *Jody Williams*
- *Terry Tempest Williams*
- *Howard Zinn*

AMERICANS WHO TELL THE TRUTH

BY ROBERT SHETTERLY

DUTTON CHILDREN'S BOOKS

New York

DUTTON CHILDREN'S BOOKS A division of Penguin Young Readers Group
Published by the Penguin Group • Penguin Group (USA) Inc., 375 Hudson Street, New York, New York 10014, U.S.A.
Penguin Group (Canada), 10 Alcorn Avenue, Toronto, Ontario, Canada M4V 3B2 (a division of Pearson Penguin Canada Inc.)
Penguin Books Ltd, 80 Strand, London WC2R 0RL, England • Penguin Ireland, 25 St Stephen's Green, Dublin 2, Ireland (a division of Penguin Books Ltd)
Penguin Group (Australia), 250 Camberwell Road, Camberwell, Victoria 3124, Australia (a division of Pearson Australia Group Pty Ltd)
Penguin Books India Pvt Ltd, 11 Community Centre, Panchsheel Park, New Delhi - 110 017, India • Penguin Group (NZ), Cnr Airborne and Rosedale Roads, Albany, Auckland 1310, New Zealand (a division of Pearson New Zealand Ltd) • Penguin Books (South Africa) (Pty) Ltd, 24 Sturdee Avenue, Rosebank, Johannesburg 2196, South Africa • Penguin Books Ltd, Registered Offices: 80 Strand, London WC2R 0RL, England

Library of Congress Cataloging-in-Publication Data

Shetterly, Robert.
Americans who tell the truth/Robert Shetterly.—1st ed.
p. cm.
ISBN 0-525-47429-3
1. United States—Biography—Juvenile literature. 2. Social reformers—United States—Biography—Juvenile literature. 3. Political activists—United States—Biography—Juvenile literature. I. Title.
CT214.S48 2005
920.073—dc22 2004024526

Published in the United States by Dutton Children's Books,
a division of Penguin Young Readers Group
345 Hudson Street, New York, New York 10014
www.penguin.com/youngreaders

Designed by Irene Vandervoort

Manufactured in China
First Edition
10 9 8 7 6 5 4 3

The law will never make men free; it is men who have got to make the law free.
— **Henry David Thoreau**

✦ ✦ ✦ ✦ ✦ ✦ ✦

Abraham Lincoln, in his Gettysburg Address, said that America is a country "... of the people, by the people, for the people." That means that we the people are responsible for our government and the action it takes, the future it envisions, the history it writes. We cannot fulfill our duty if we don't know the truth. Many of the people in these paintings have dedicated their lives to uncovering the truth so that when we give our consent it is truly informed. They are some of the Americans who tell the truth.

Often it takes great courage to stand up to people in the government or the press and demand the truth. All of us must ask ourselves what it means to be patriotic. Does it mean obeying people in powerful positions and doing whatever they ask us to do? Or does it mean discovering for ourselves what truly serves the common good, the hope for justice, and the real ideals of America? We must remember that, in a democracy, the people have the rights, not the government.

Many of the people in this book have been called unpatriotic. Their struggles to uncover the truth have been criticized. Attempts have been made to discredit them and, often, their lives have been threatened. But these are the people who love the idea of America and the promise of equality it offers to all.

By saying that these are some Americans who tell the truth, I mean that they are concerned with the maintenance of democracy, with a social organization that cares for the fundamental dignity and equal worth of every individual. They defend the right of every citizen to have the opportunity for a good education, a safe workplace, good health care, a sustainable environment, and an equal chance to participate in the great cultural and social wealth of this society. They believe that until all of us are free, none of us are free. They also believe that one of the responsibilities of living in a democracy is the obligation of every person to work toward that goal, and that honest dissent is necessary so that the people can give their honest consent. Just as there will always be people who struggle for justice, there will always be those who try to take it away. Dissent is the necessary part of this equation.

Their courage in standing up for the promise of America can give us all the hope and courage to stand up for it ourselves. History is not just something that we read about or that happens *to* us. History is something we shape by our determination to be involved in the events of our time. All of us, adults and children, can have an effect on our history by insisting that our questions are answered, the truth is told, and that we are passing on to future generations a more just and equal world.

—Robert Shetterly

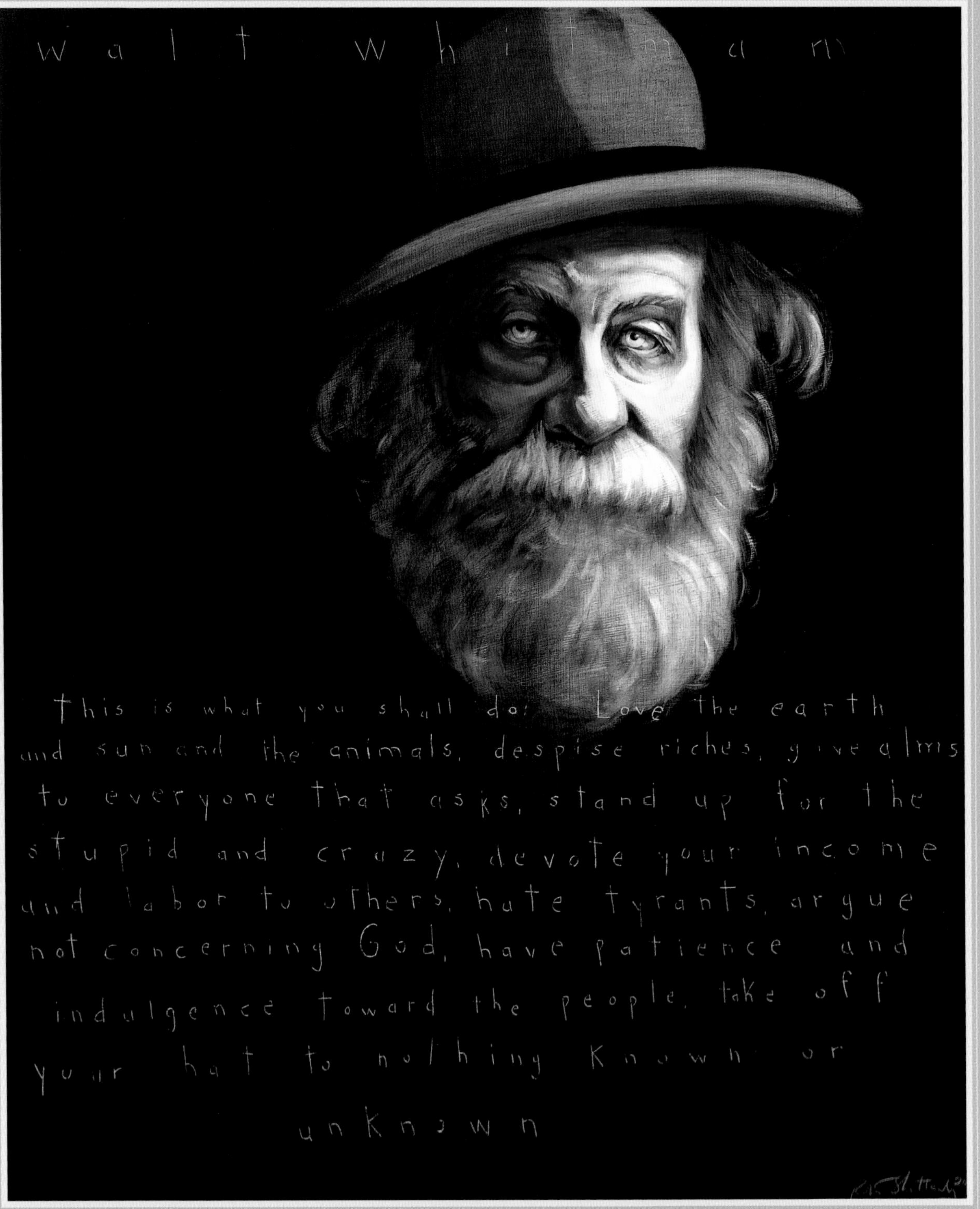

Walt Whitman

American poet, 1819–1892

This is what you shall do: Love the earth and sun and the animals, despise riches, give alms to everyone that asks, stand up for the stupid and crazy, devote your income and labor to others, hate tyrants, argue not concerning God, have patience and indulgence toward the people, take off your hat to nothing known or unknown.

Samantha Smith

Grade-school student, peace activist, 1972–1985

If we could be friends by just getting to know each other better, then what are our countries really arguing about? Nothing could be more important than not *having a war if a war could kill everything.*

Marian Wright Edelman

Children's advocate, 1939–

What's wrong with our children? –Adults telling children to be honest while lying and cheating. Adults telling children not to be violent while marketing and glorifying violence. . . I believe that adult hypocrisy is the biggest problem children face in America.

Sojourner Truth

Abolitionist, evangelist, feminist, 1797–1883

Now I hears talkin' about de Constitution and de rights of man. I comes up and I takes hold of dis Constitution. It looks mighty big, and I feels for my rights, but der aint any dare. Den I says, God, what ails dis Constitution? He says to me, "Sojourner, dere is a little weasel in it."

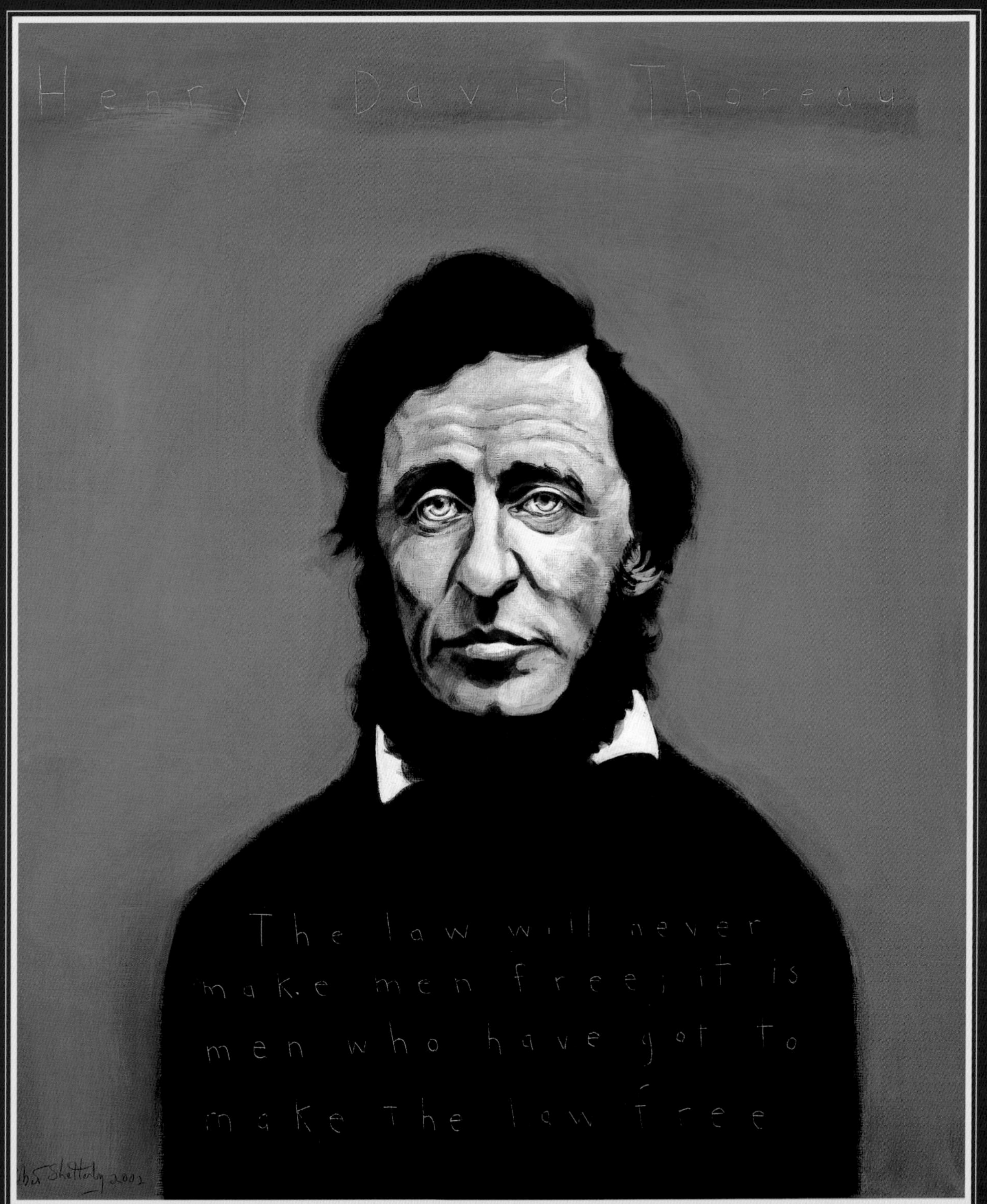
Henry David Thoreau
The law will never
make men free; it is
men who have got to
make the law free

5

Henry David Thoreau

Naturalist, writer, social critic, 1817–1862

The law will never make men free; it is men who have got to make the law free.

Mark Twain

Writer, humorist, social critic, 1835–1910

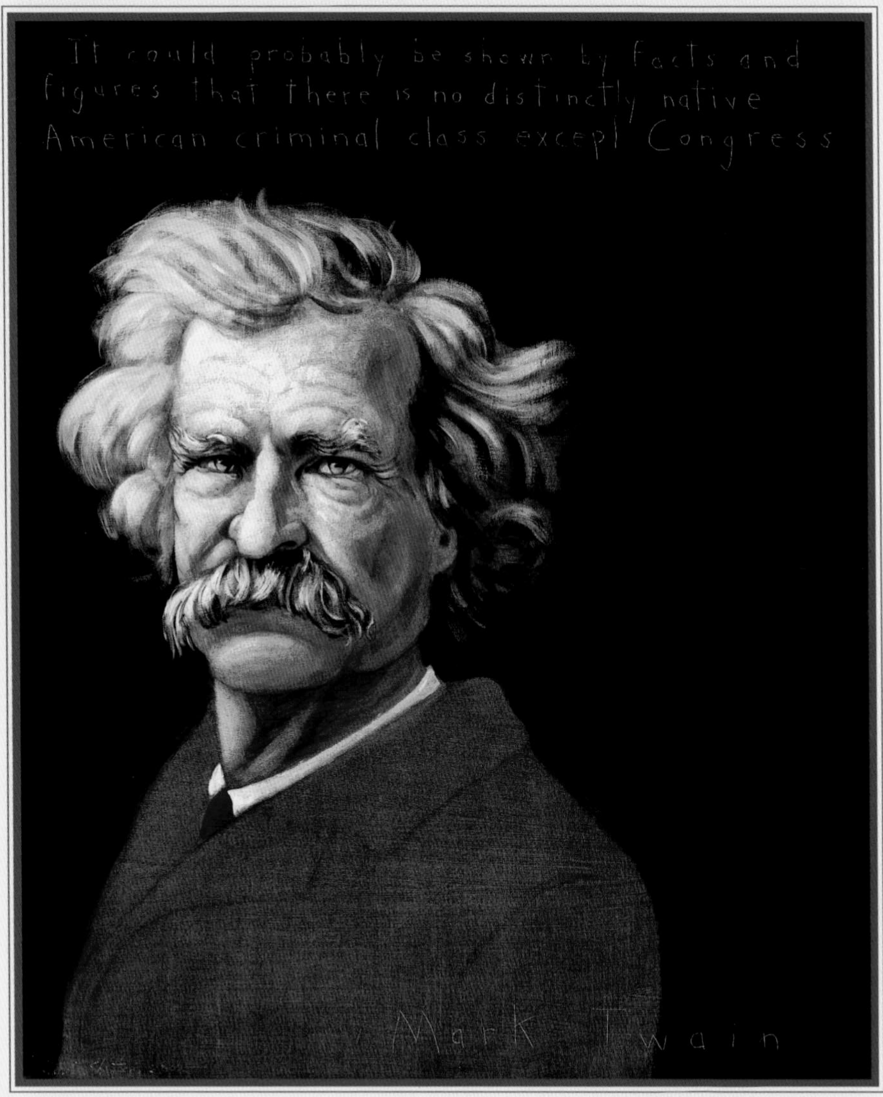
It could probably be shown by facts and figures that there is no distinctly native American criminal class except Congress
Mark Twain

It could probably be shown by facts and figures that there is no distinctly native American criminal class except Congress.

John Muir

Conservationist, naturalist, explorer, 1838–1914

The battle we have fought, and are still fighting for the forests is part of the eternal conflict between right and wrong, and we cannot expect to see the end of it . . . So we must count on watching and striving for these trees, and should always be glad to find anything so surely good and noble to strive for.
John Muir

The battle we have fought, and are still fighting for the forests is part of the eternal conflict between right and wrong, and we cannot expect to see the end of it . . . So we must count on watching and striving for these trees, and should always be glad to find anything so surely good and noble to strive for.

Frederick
Douglass
Where justice is denied, where poverty is
enforced, where ignorance prevails, and where
any one class is made to feel that society is
in an organized conspiracy to oppress, rob,
and degrade them, neither persons nor
property will be safe.

Frederick Douglass

Antislavery orator and writer, 1818–1895

Where justice is denied, where poverty is enforced, where ignorance prevails, and where any one class is made to feel that society is an organized conspiracy to oppress, rob, and degrade them, neither persons nor property will be safe.

(Speech on the 24th anniversary of Emancipation, Washington, D.C.)

Chief Joseph

Native American leader, c. 1840–1904

I have asked some of the great white chiefs where they get their authority to say to the Indian that he shall stay in one place, while he sees white men going where they please. They can not tell me.

Jane Addams

Social reformer, 1860–1935

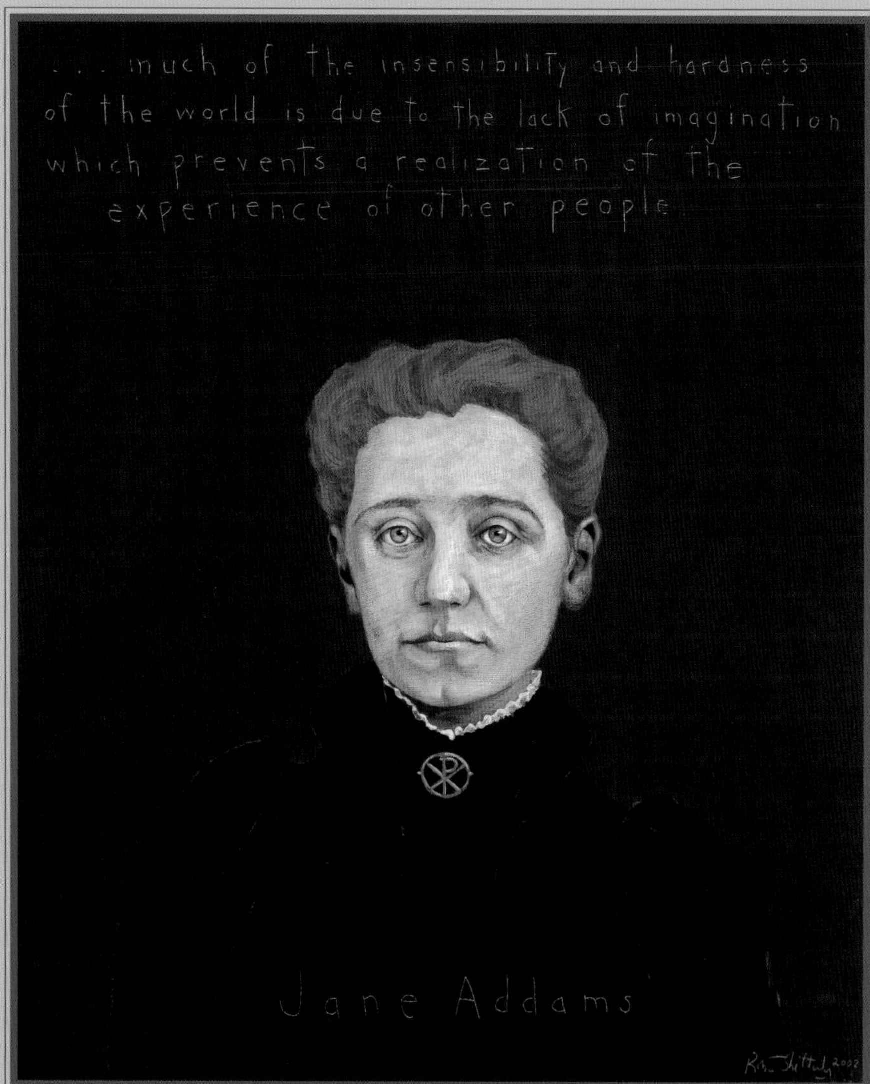

Much of the insensibility and hardness of the world is due to the lack of imagination which prevents a realization of the experience of other people.

Dorothy Day

Social activist, journalist, 1897–1980

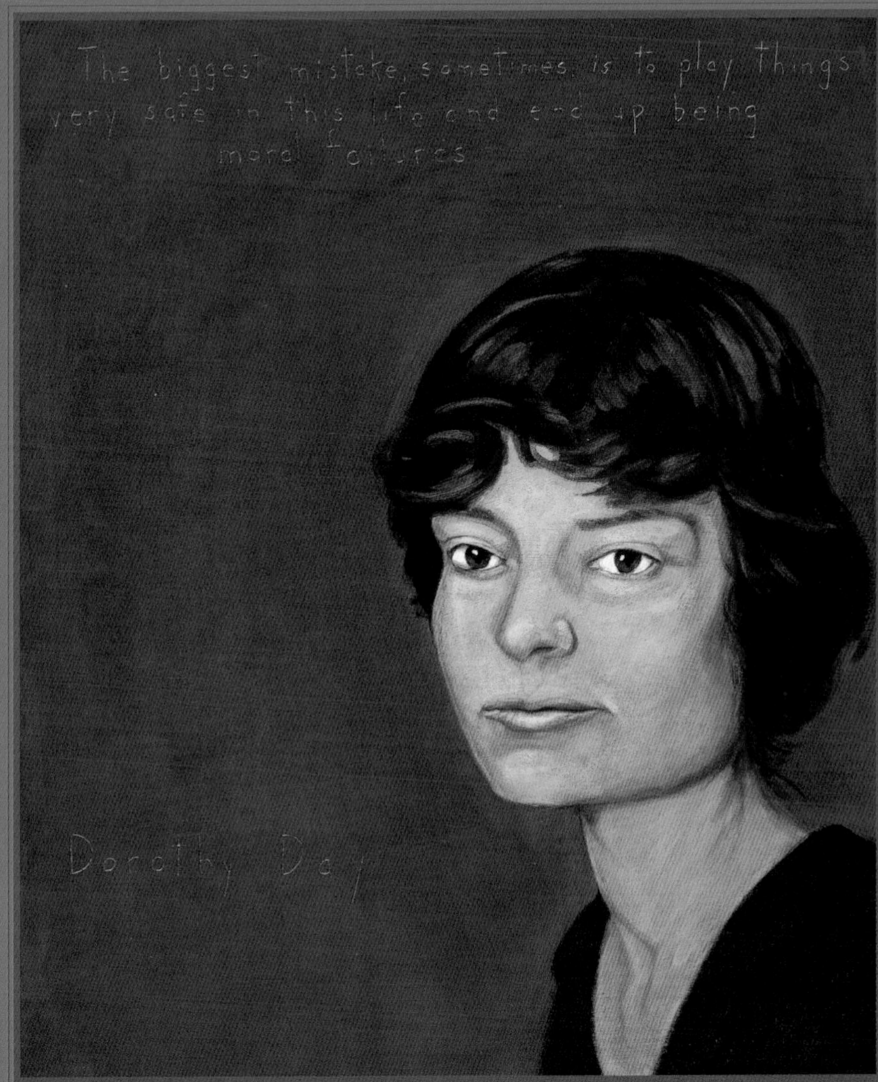

The biggest mistake sometimes is to play things very safe in this life and end up being moral failures.

W.E.B. Du Bois

Writer, teacher, civil-rights spokesperson, 1868–1963

Back of the problem of race and color lies a greater problem . . . and that is the fact that so many civilized persons are willing to live in comfort even if the price of this is poverty, ignorance, and disease of the majority of their fellowmen; that to maintain this privilege men have waged war until today war tends to become universal and continuous.

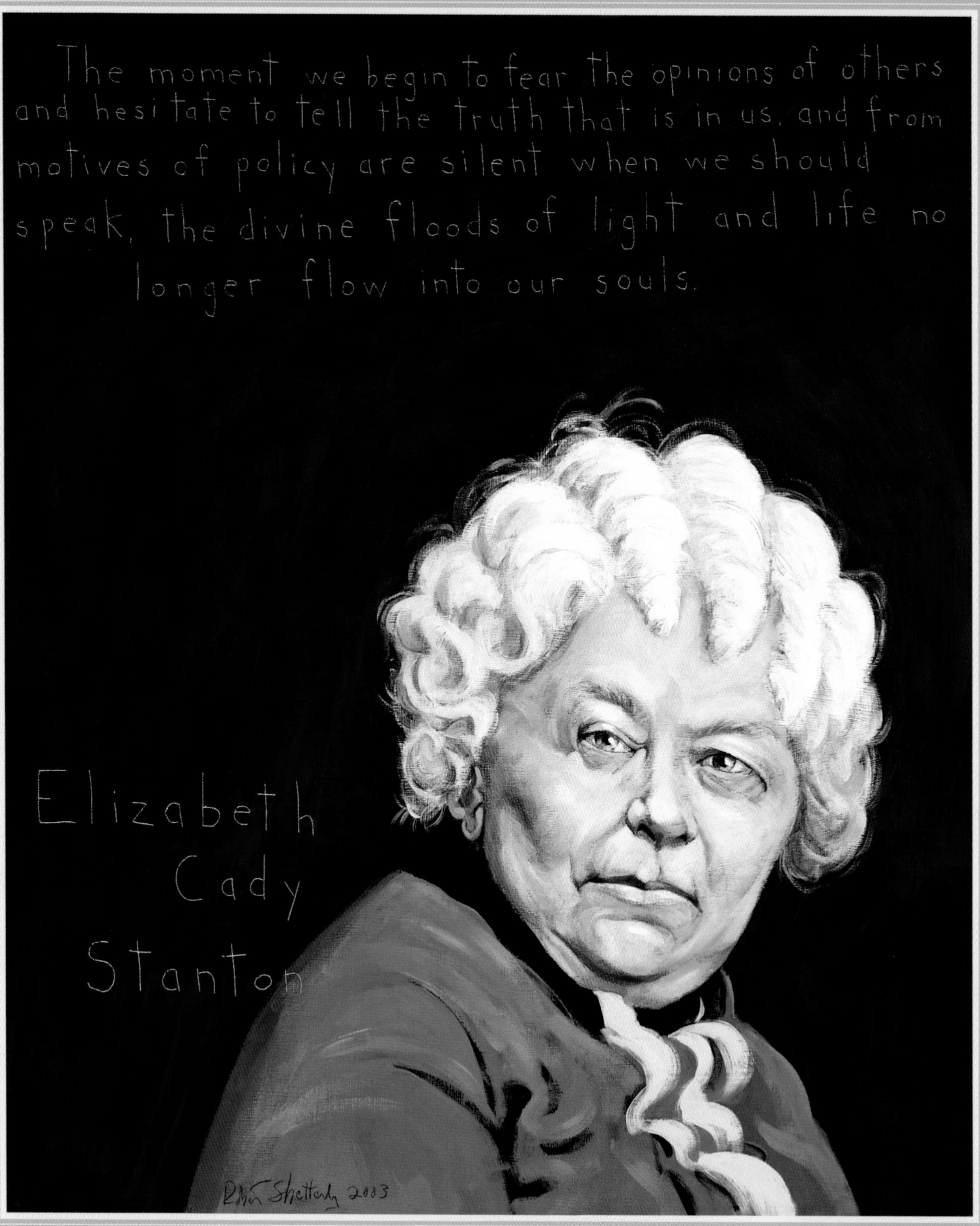

ELIZABETH CADY STANTON

Reformer, writer, lecturer, 1815–1902

The moment we begin to fear the opinions of others and hesitate to tell the truth that is in us, and from motives of policy are silent when we should speak, the divine floods of light and life no longer flow into our souls.

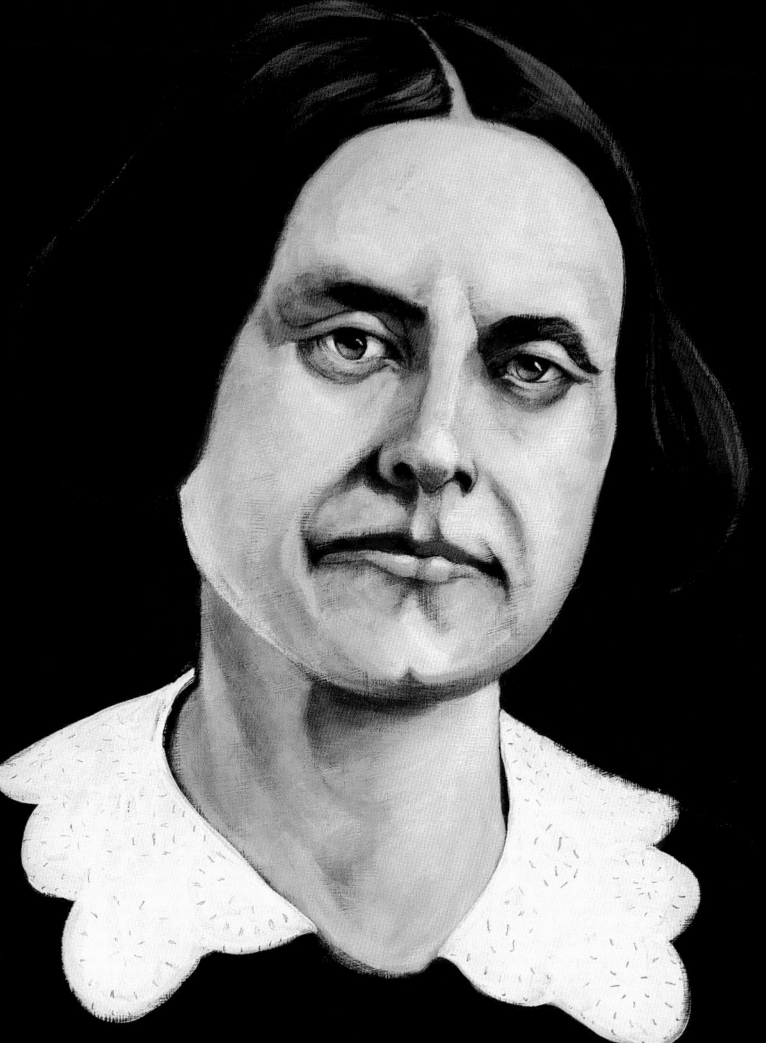
Susan B Anthony
Women, we might as well be dogs baying the
moon as petitioners without the right
to vote!

SUSAN B. ANTHONY

Reformer, women's suffrage leader, 1820–1906

Women, we might as well be dogs baying the moon as petitioners without the right to vote!

Rosa Parks

Seamstress, civil-rights leader, 1913–

The only tired I was, was tired of giving in.

Ida B. Wells

Journalist, antilynching crusader, women's-rights advocate, 1862–1931

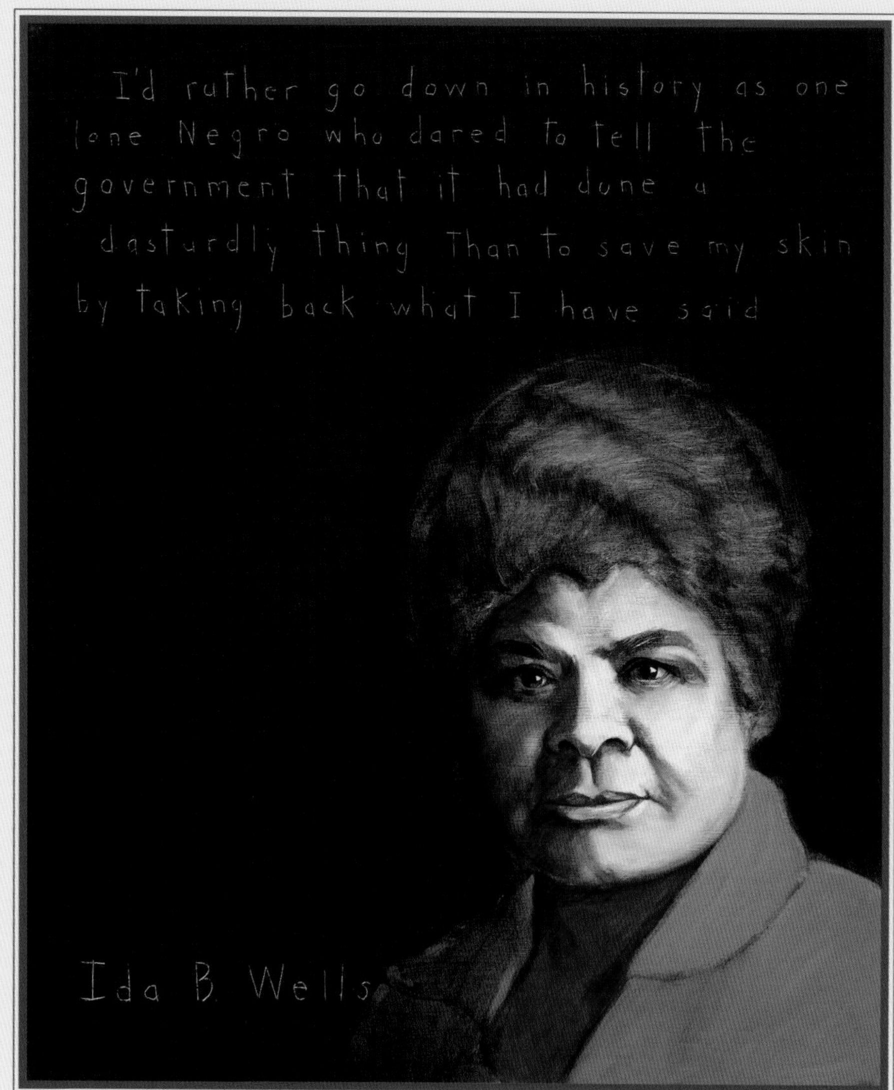

I'd rather go down in history as one lone Negro who dared to tell the government that it had done a dastardly thing than to save my skin by taking back what I said.

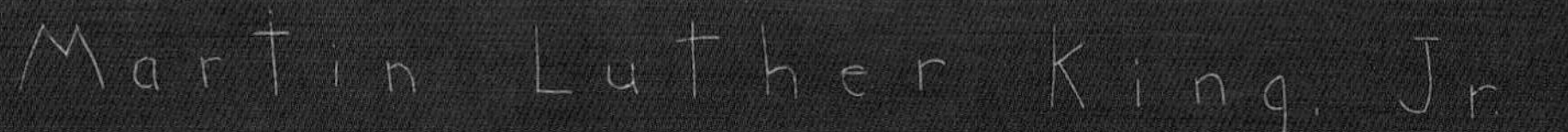
Martin Luther King, Jr.

Nonviolence is a powerful
and just weapon . . . which cuts
without wounding and ennobles
the man who wields it. It is a
sword that heals.

Martin Luther King, Jr.

Clergyman, civil-rights leader, 1929–1968

Non-violence is a powerful and just weapon which cuts without wounding and ennobles the man who wields it. It is a sword that heals.

Mary Harris "Mother" Jones

Labor leader, organizer, 1830–1930

Goodbye, boys; I'm under arrest. I may have to go to jail. I may not see you for a long time. Keep up the fight! Don't surrender! Pay no attention to the injunction machine at Parkersburg. The Federal judge is a scab anyhow. While you starve he plays golf. While you serve humanity, he serves injunctions for the money powers.

Goodbye, boys; I'm under arrest. I may have to go to jail. I may not see you for a long time. Keep up the fight! Don't surrender! Pay no attention to the injunction machine at Parkersburg. The Federal judge is a scab anyhow. While you starve he plays golf. While you serve humanity, he serves injunctions for the money powers.

Mother Jones

Cesar Chavez

Founder of farm workers' union, human-rights activist, 1927–1993

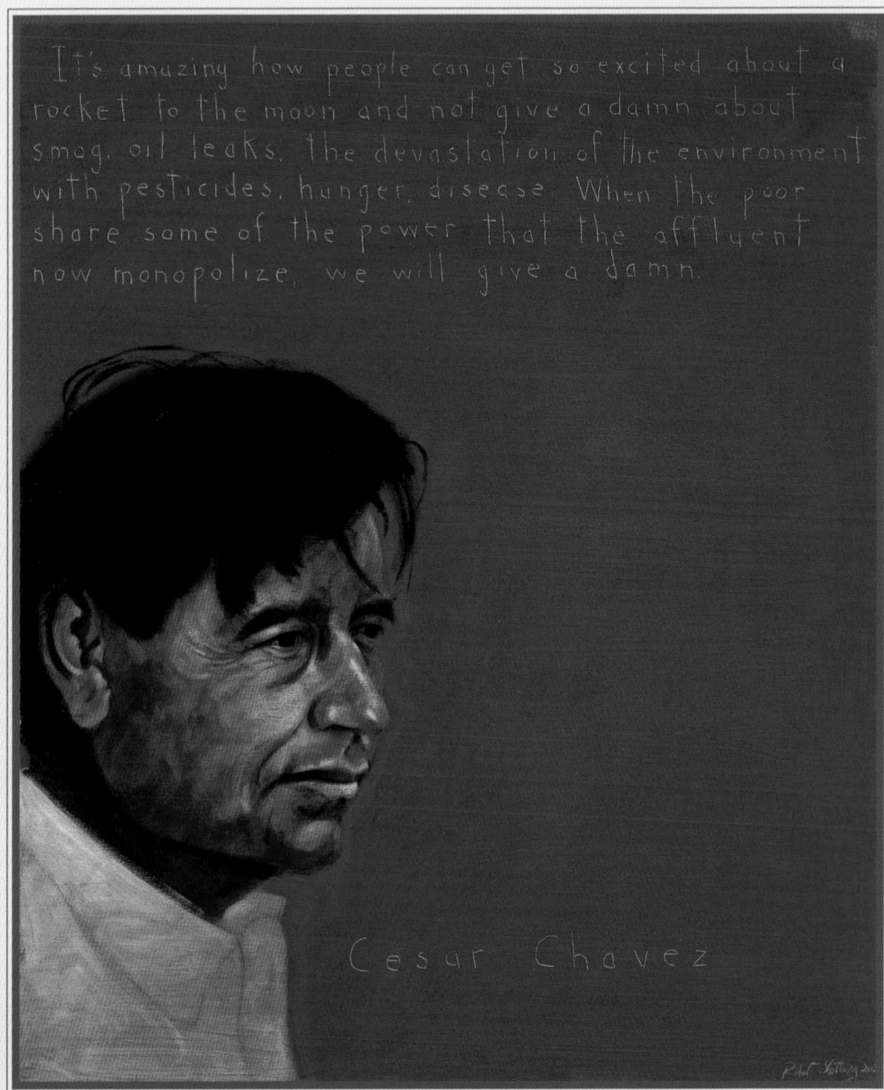

It's amazing how people can get so excited about a rocket to the moon and not give a damn about smog, oil leaks, the devastation of the environment with pesticides, hunger, disease. When the poor share some of the power that the affluent now monopolize, we will give a damn.

James Baldwin

Fiction writer, essayist, social critic, 1924–1987

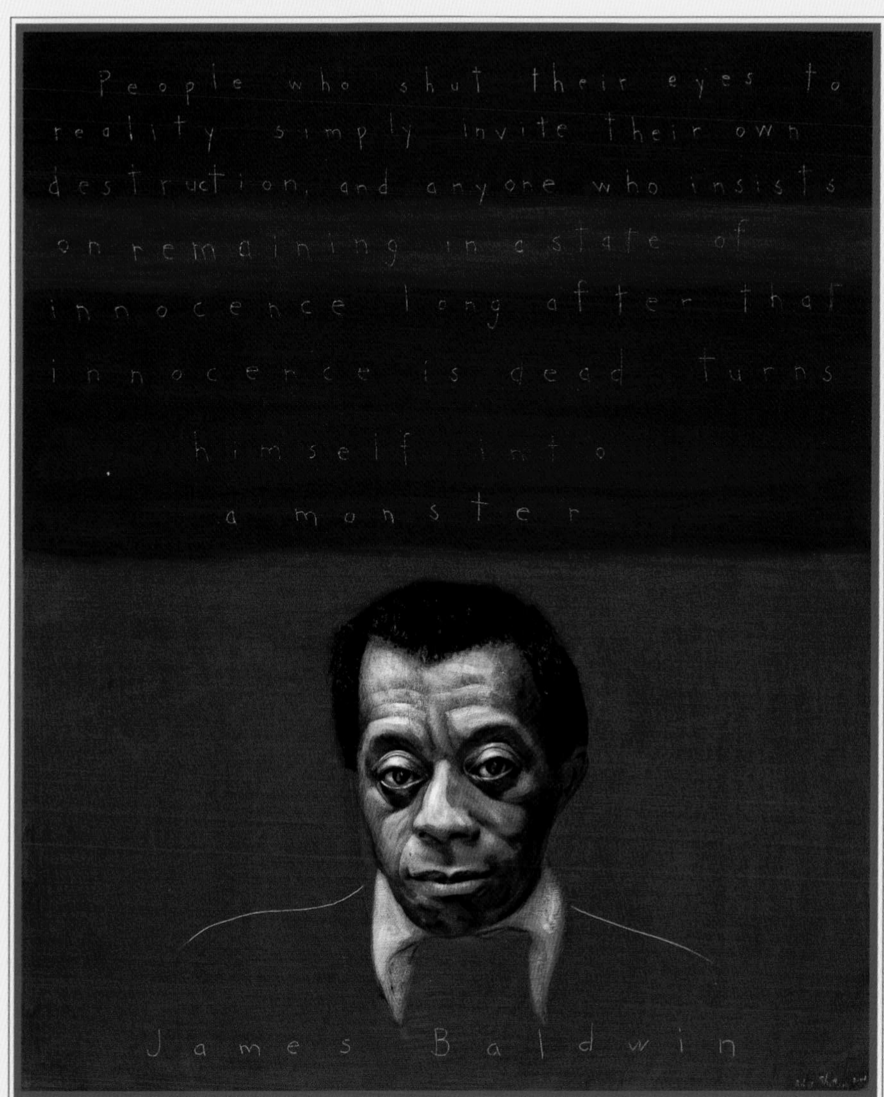

People who shut their eyes to reality simply invite their own destruction, and anyone who insists on remaining in a state of innocence long after that innocence is dead turns himself into a monster.

The rule of law does not do away with the unequal distribution of wealth and power, but reinforces that inequality with the authority of law. It allocates wealth and poverty . . . in such complicated and indirect ways as to leave the victim bewildered.

Howard Zinn

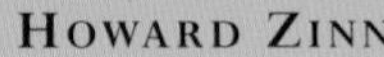

Howard Zinn

Historian, political theorist, educator, 1922–

The rule of law does not do away with the unequal distribution of wealth and power, but reinforces that inequality with the authority of law. It allocates wealth and poverty . . . in such calculated and indirect ways as to leave the victim bewildered.

17

Emma Goldman

Anarchist, feminist, labor advocate, 1869–1940

The greatest bulwark of capitalism is militarism.

Eleanor Roosevelt

Humanitarian, social reformer, 1884–1962

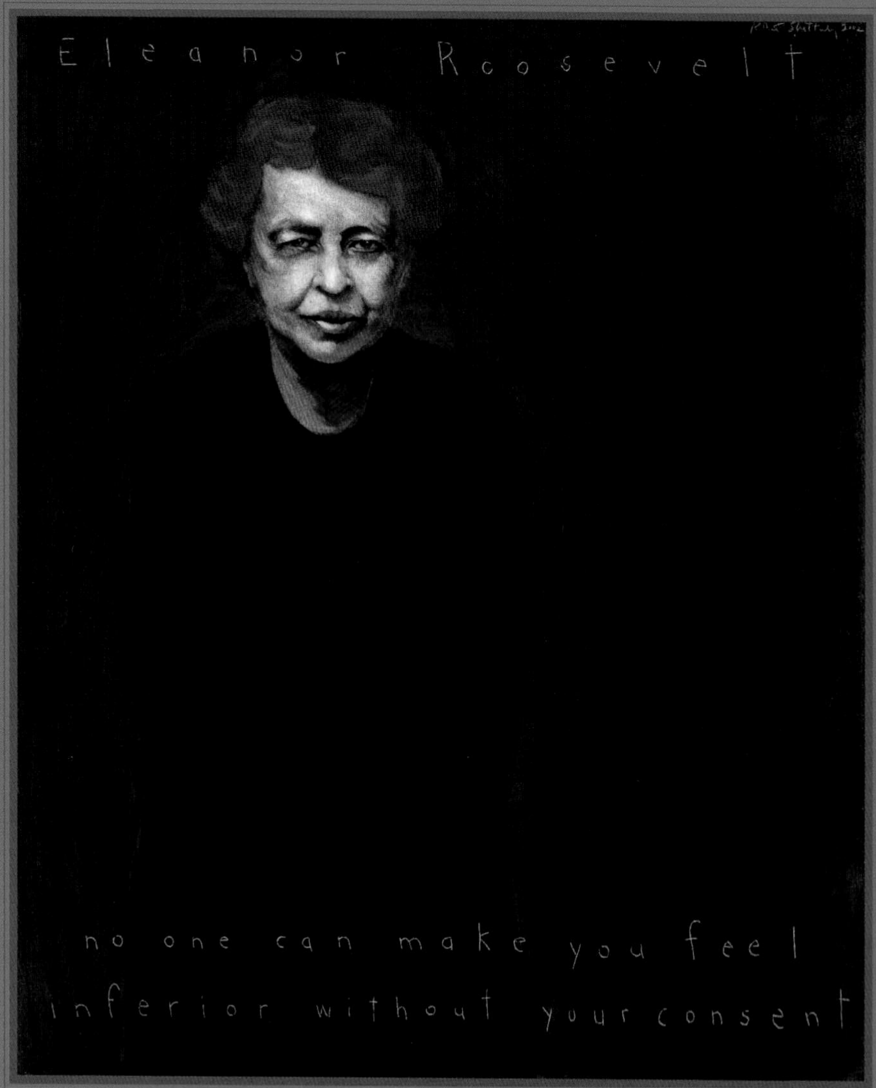

No one can make you feel inferior without your consent.

Margaret Chase Smith

United States senator, 1897–1995

The right to criticize; the right to hold unpopular beliefs; the right to protest; the right of independent thought. The exercise of these rights should not cost one single American citizen his reputation or his right to a livelihood... Otherwise none of us could call our souls our own.

Woody Guthrie

Folksinger, writer, 1912–1967

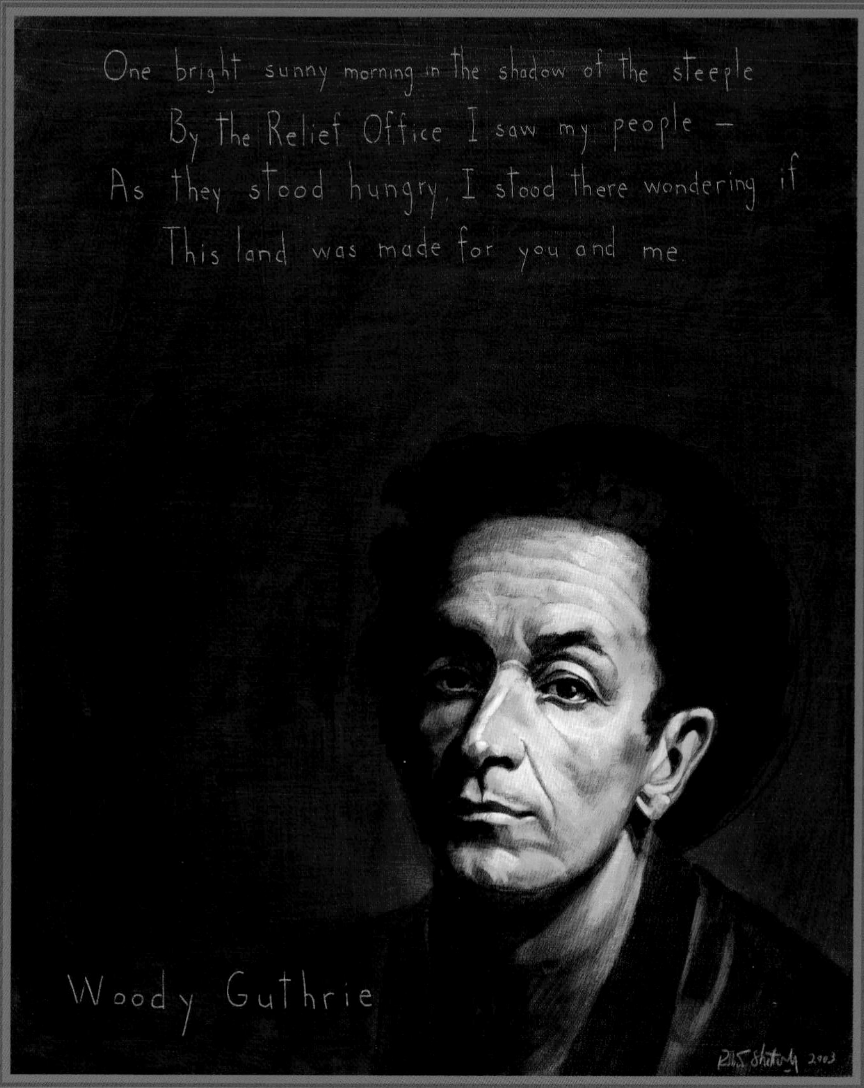

One bright sunny morning in the shadow of the steeple
By the Relief Office I saw my people –
As they stood hungry, I stood there wondering if
This land was made for you and me.
Woody Guthrie

One bright sunny morning in the shadow of the steeple / By the Relief Office I saw my people— As they stood hungry, I stood there wondering if / This land was made for you and me.

Paul Robeson

Singer, writer, civil-rights activist, 1898–1976

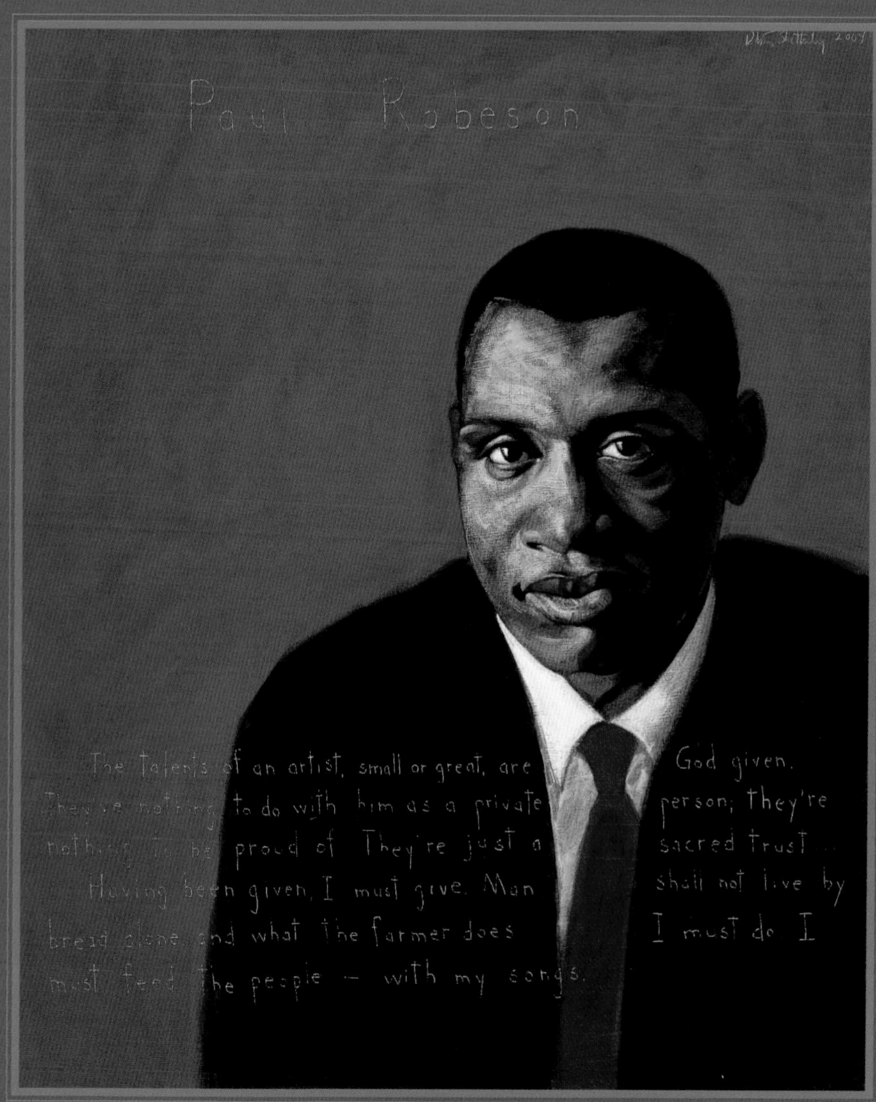

Paul Robeson

The talents of an artist, small or great, are God given. They've nothing to do with him as a private person; they're nothing to be proud of. They're just a sacred trust… Having been given, I must give. Man shall not live by bread alone, and what the farmer does I must do. I must feed the people— with my songs.

Zora Neale Hurston

Author, folklorist, 1891–1960

"So de white man throw down de load and tell de nigger man tuh pick it up. He pick it up because he have to, but he don't tote it. He hand it to his womenfolks. De nigger woman is de mule uh de world so fur as Ah can see. Ah been prayin' fuh it tuh be different wid you. Lawd, Lawd, Lawd!"

(Nanny in *Their Eyes Were Watching God*)

Dwight Eisenhower

Military leader, president of the United States, 1890–1969

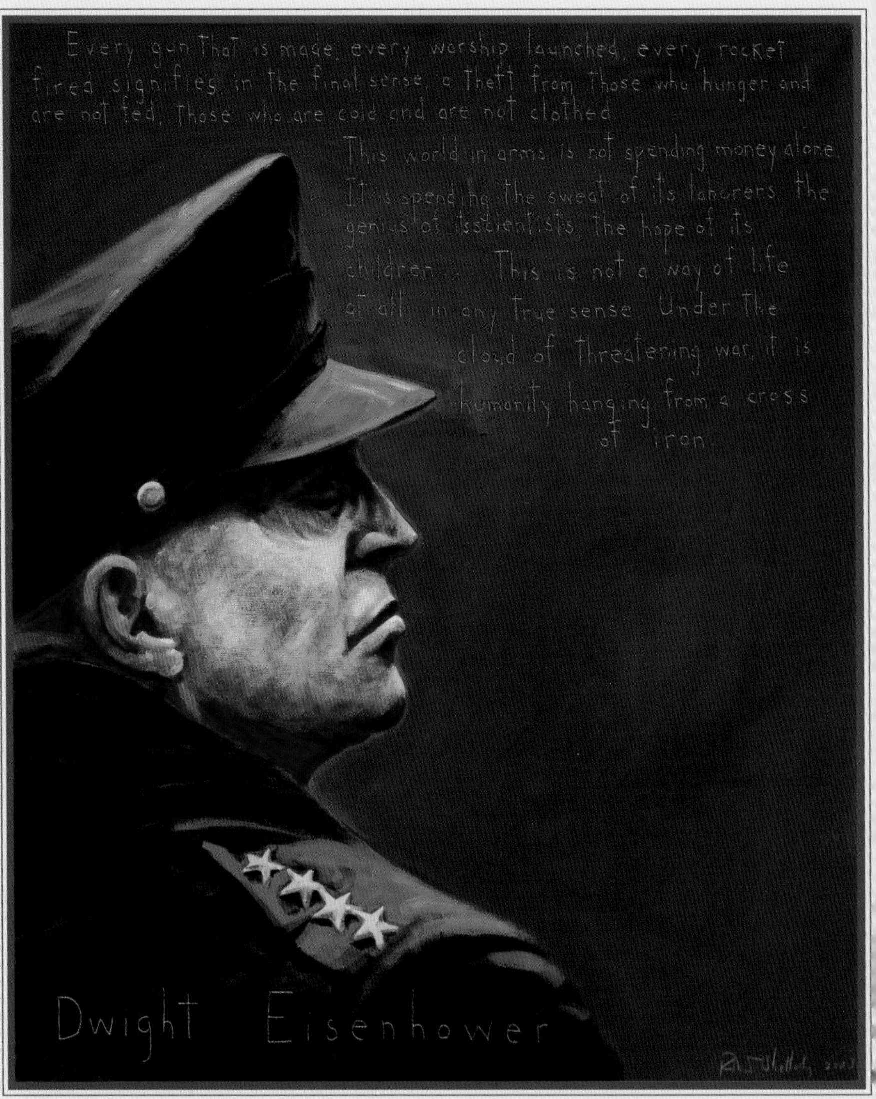

Every gun that is made, every warship launched, every rocket fired signifies, in the final sense, a theft from those who hunger and are not fed, those who are cold and are not clothed. The world in arms is not spending money alone. It is spending the sweat of its laborers, the genius of its scientists, the hope of its children…This is not a way of life at all, in any true sense. Under the cloud of threatening war, it is humanity hanging from a cross of iron.

(Speech delivered before the American Society of Newspaper Editors, Washington, D.C., April 16, 1953)

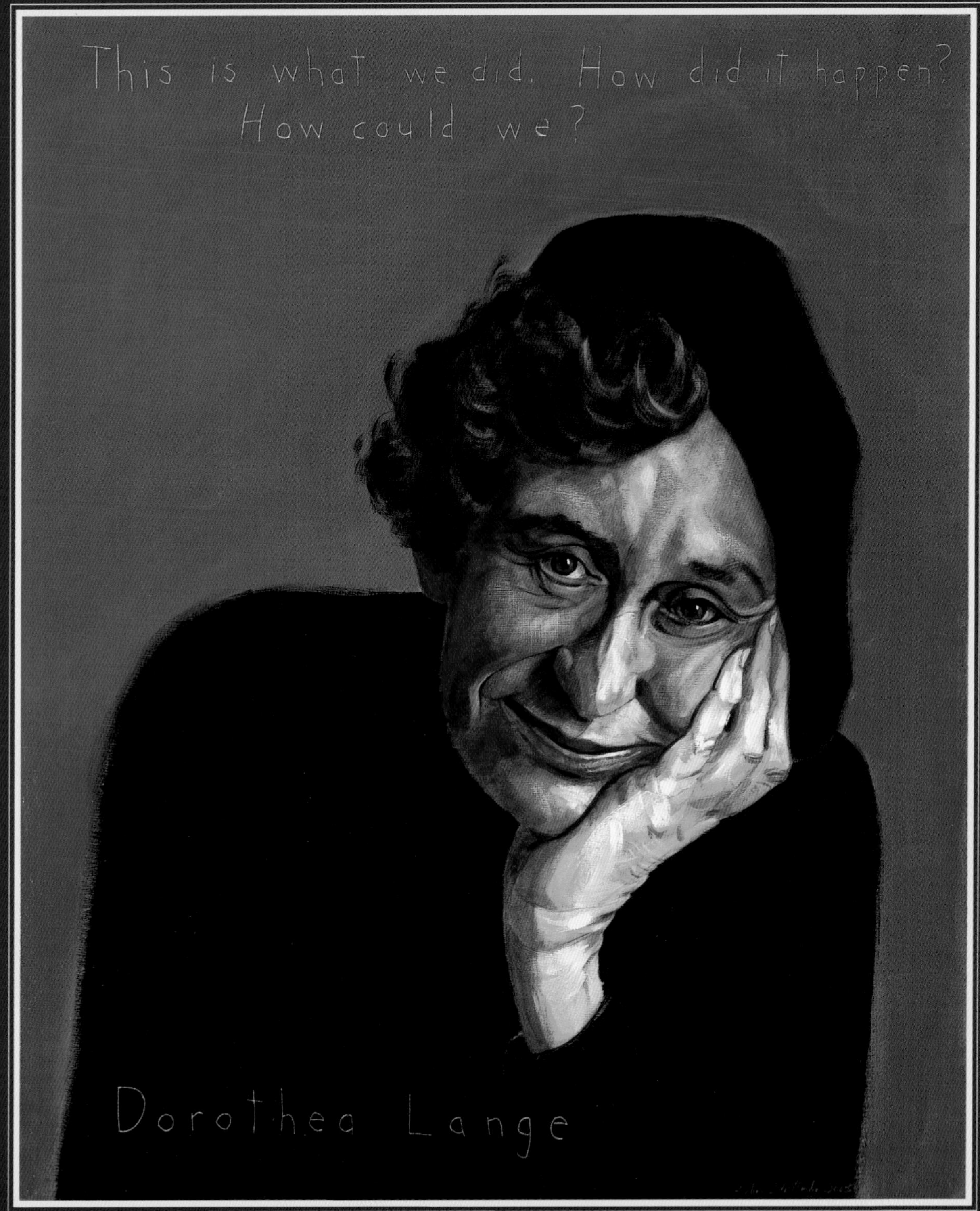
This is what we did. How did it happen?
How could we?
Dorothea Lange

21

Dorothea Lange

Photographer, 1895–1965

This is what we did. How did it happen?
How could we?

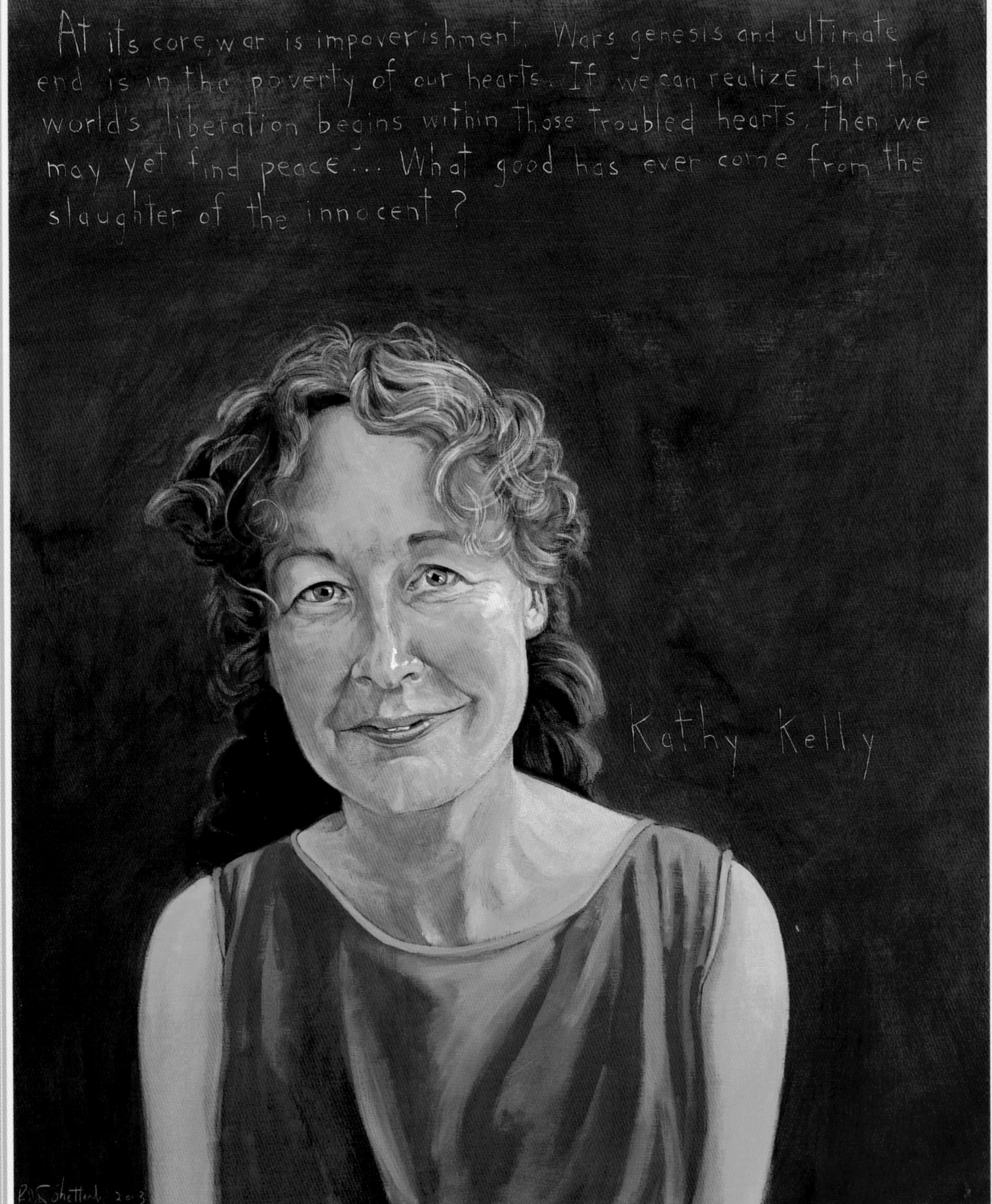
At its core, war is impoverishment. Wars genesis and ultimate
end is in the poverty of our hearts. If we can realize that the
world's liberation begins within those troubled hearts, then we
may yet find peace... What good has ever come from the
slaughter of the innocent?
Kathy Kelly

Kathy Kelly

Peace activist, 1953–

At its core, war is impoverishment. War's genesis and ultimate end is in the poverty of our hearts. If we can realize that the world's liberation begins within those troubled hearts, then we may yet find peace... What good has ever come from the slaughter of the innocent?

Noam Chomsky

Linguist, political activist, writer, 1928–

Jingoism, racism, fear, religious fundamentalism: these are the ways of appealing to people if you're trying to organize a mass base of support for policies that are really intended to crush them.

Muhammad Ali

Boxer, 1942–

If I thought going to war would bring freedom and equality to twenty-two million of my people, they wouldn't have to draft me. I'd join tomorrow. But I either have to obey the laws of the land or the laws of Allah. I have nothing to lose by standing up and following my beliefs. We've been in jail for four hundred years.

Rachel Carson

the "control of nature" is a phrase conceived in arrogance, born of the Neanderthal age of biology and the convenience of man.

Rachel Carson

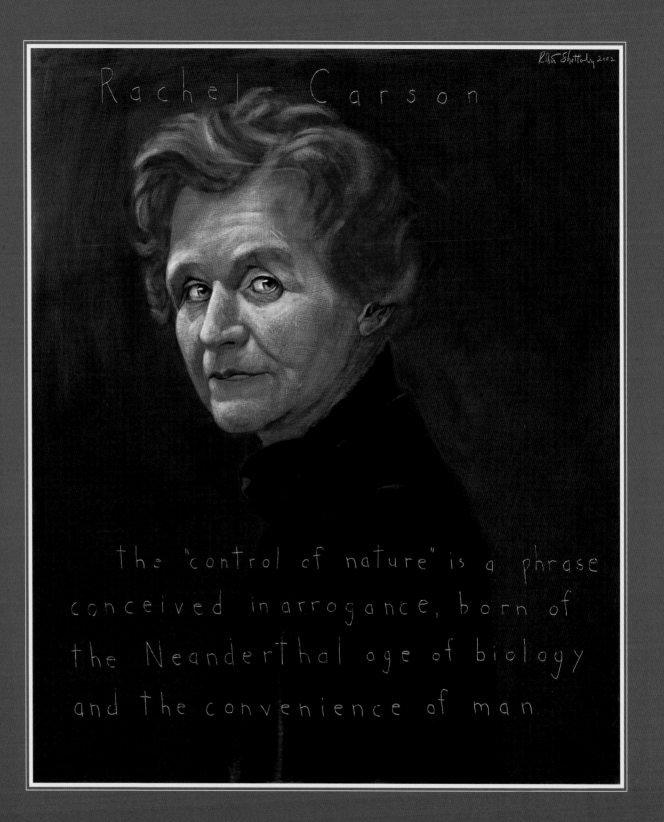

Biologist, writer, ecologist, 1907–1964

The "control of nature" is a phrase conceived in arrogance, born of the Neanderthal age of biology and the convenience of man.

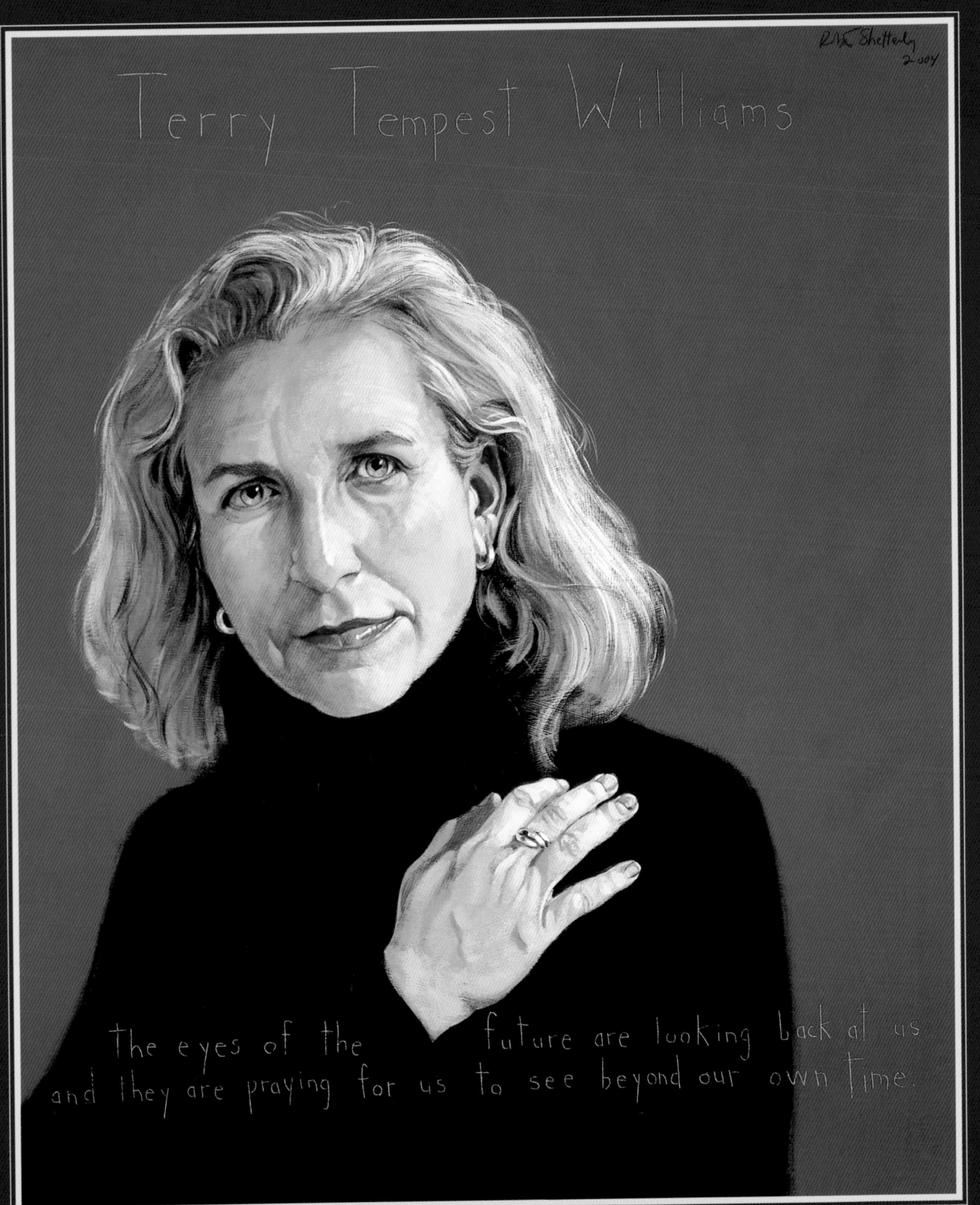
RWS Shetterly
2004
Terry Tempest Williams
The eyes of the future are looking back at us
and they are praying for us to see beyond our own time.

Terry Tempest Williams
Writer, environmentalist, activist, 1955–

The eyes of the future are looking back at us and they are praying for us to see beyond our own time.

RALPH NADER

Public citizen, 1934–

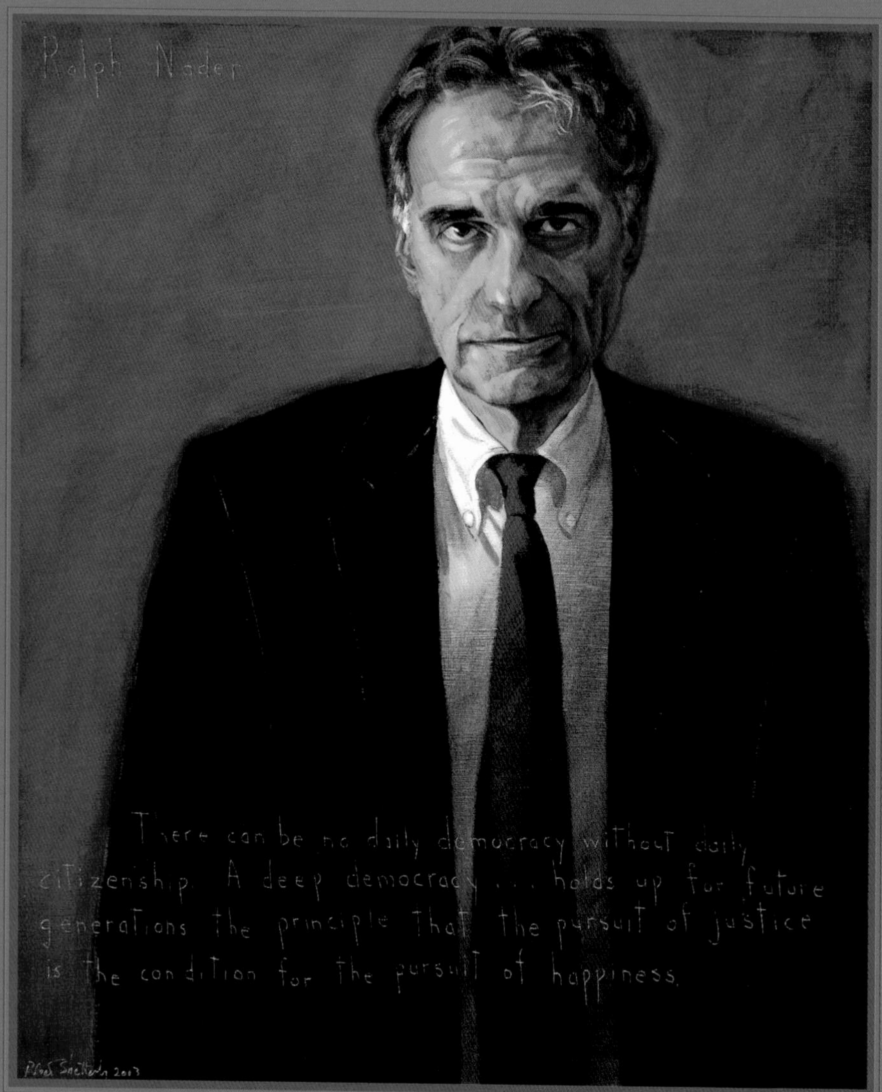

There can be no daily democracy without daily citizenship. A deep democracy . . . holds up for future generations the principle that the pursuit of justice is the condition for the pursuit of happiness.

HELEN KELLER

Writer, lecturer, activist, advocate for the disabled, 1880–1968

When one comes to think of it, there are no such things as divine, immutable, or inalienable rights. Rights are things we get when we are strong enough to make good our claim on them.

Molly Ivins

Political columnist, 1944–

The best way to get the sons of bitches is to make people laugh at them.

Jim Hightower

Former Texas politician, author, speaker, 1943–

The opposite of courage is not cowardice, it is conformity. Even a dead fish can go with the flow.

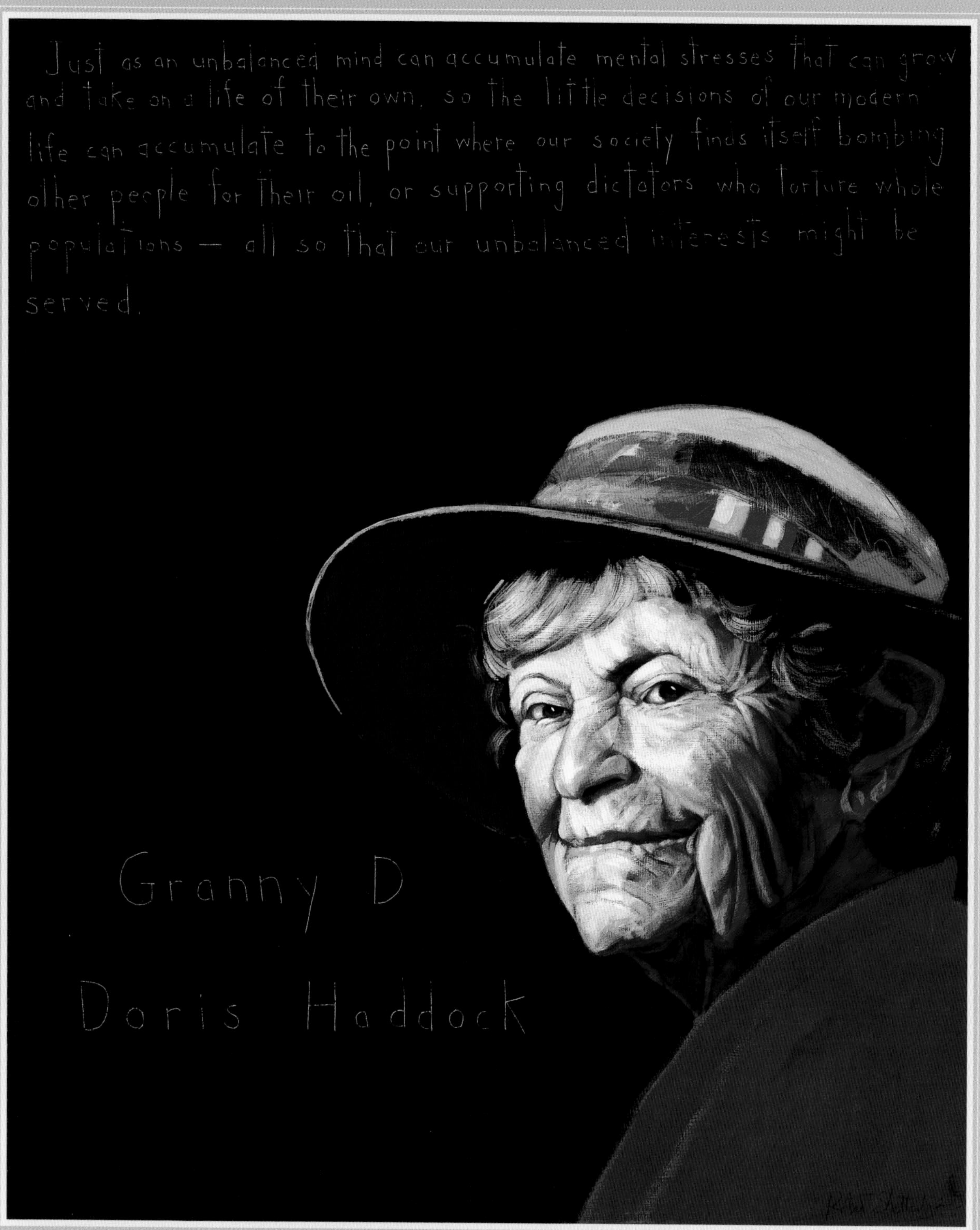
Just as an unbalanced mind can accumulate mental stresses that can grow
and take on a life of their own, so the little decisions of our modern
life can accumulate to the point where our society finds itself bombing
other people for their oil, or supporting dictators who torture whole
populations — all so that our unbalanced interests might be
served.
Granny D
Doris Haddock

Doris Haddock ("Granny D")

Activist, 1910–

Just as an unbalanced mind can accumulate stresses that can grow and take on a life of their own, so little decisions of our modern life can accumulate to the point where our society finds itself bombing other people for their oil, or supporting dictators who torture whole populations—all so that our unbalanced interests might be served.

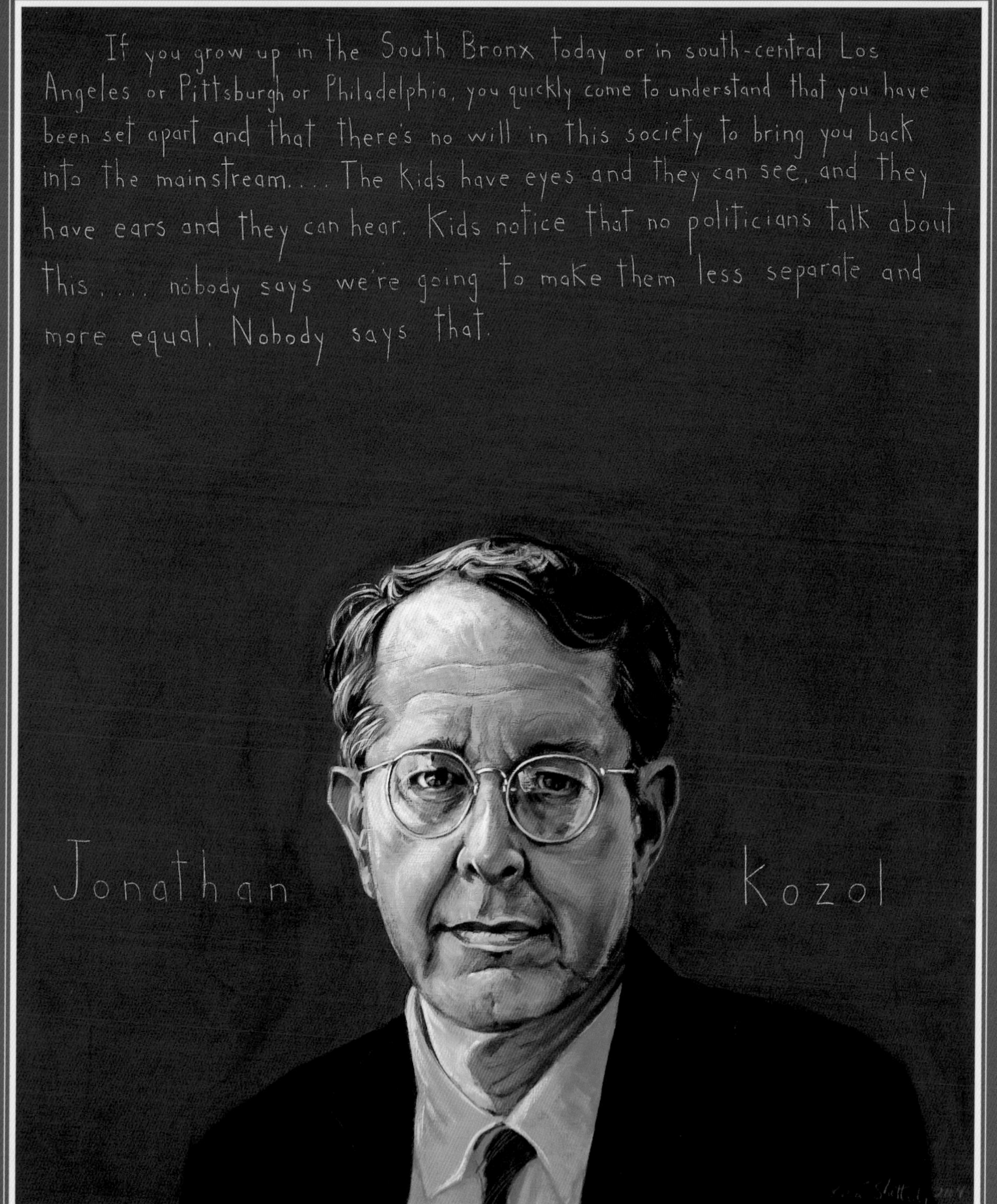
If you grow up in the South Bronx today or in south-central Los
Angeles or Pittsburgh or Philadelphia, you quickly come to understand that you have
been set apart and that there's no will in this society to bring you back
into the mainstream.... The kids have eyes and they can see, and they
have ears and they can hear. Kids notice that no politicians talk about
this.... nobody says we're going to make them less separate and
more equal. Nobody says that.
Jonathan
Kozol

JONATHAN KOZOL

Educator, writer, activist, 1936–

If you grow up in the South Bronx today or in south-central Los Angeles or Pittsburgh or Philadelphia, you quickly come to understand that you have been set apart and that there's no will in this society to bring you back into the mainstream. The kids have eyes and they can see, and they have ears and they can hear. Kids notice that no politicians talk about this. Nobody says we're going to make them less separate and more equal. Nobody says that.

30

The most alarming sign of the state of our society now is that our leaders have the courage to sacrifice the lives of young people in war but have not the courage to tell us that we must be less greedy and less wasteful.
Wendell Berry

Wendell Berry

Farmer, essayist, conservationist, novelist, teacher, poet, 1934–

The most alarming sign of the state of our society now is that our leaders have the courage to sacrifice the lives of young people in war but have not the courage to tell us that we must be less greedy and less wasteful.

Perry Mann

Teacher, lawyer, writer, 1921–

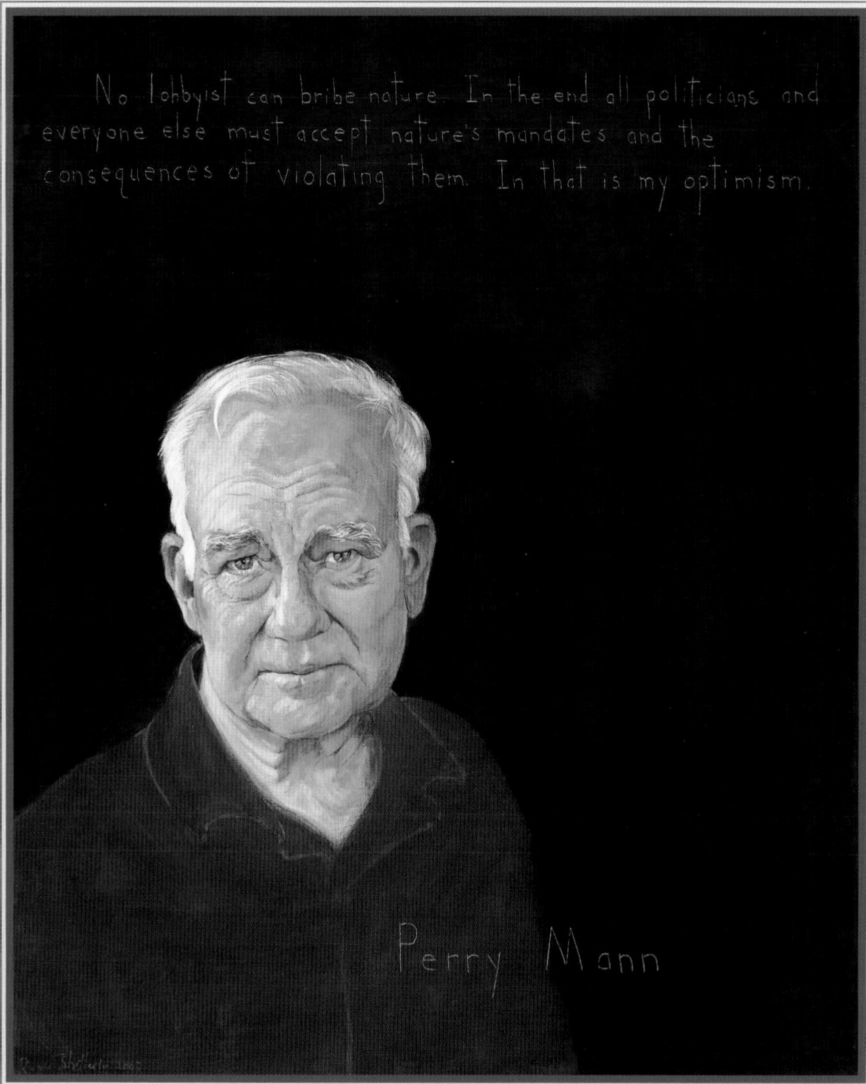

No lobbyist can bribe nature. In the end all politicians and everyone else must accept nature's mandates and the consequences of violating them. In that is my optimism.

Lewis Lapham

Journalist, magazine editor, author, 1935–

Because God had chosen America as the construction site of the earthly Paradise, America's cause was always just and nothing was ever America's fault.... corrupt foreigners commit crimes against humanity, Americans cleanse the world of its impurities.

Judy Wicks

Activist, businessperson, 1947–

I'm helping to create an economic system that will respect and protect the earth—one which would replace corporate globalization with a global network of local living economies. Business is beautiful when it's a vehicle for serving the common good.

Louis "Studs" Terkel

Author, radio personality, 1912–

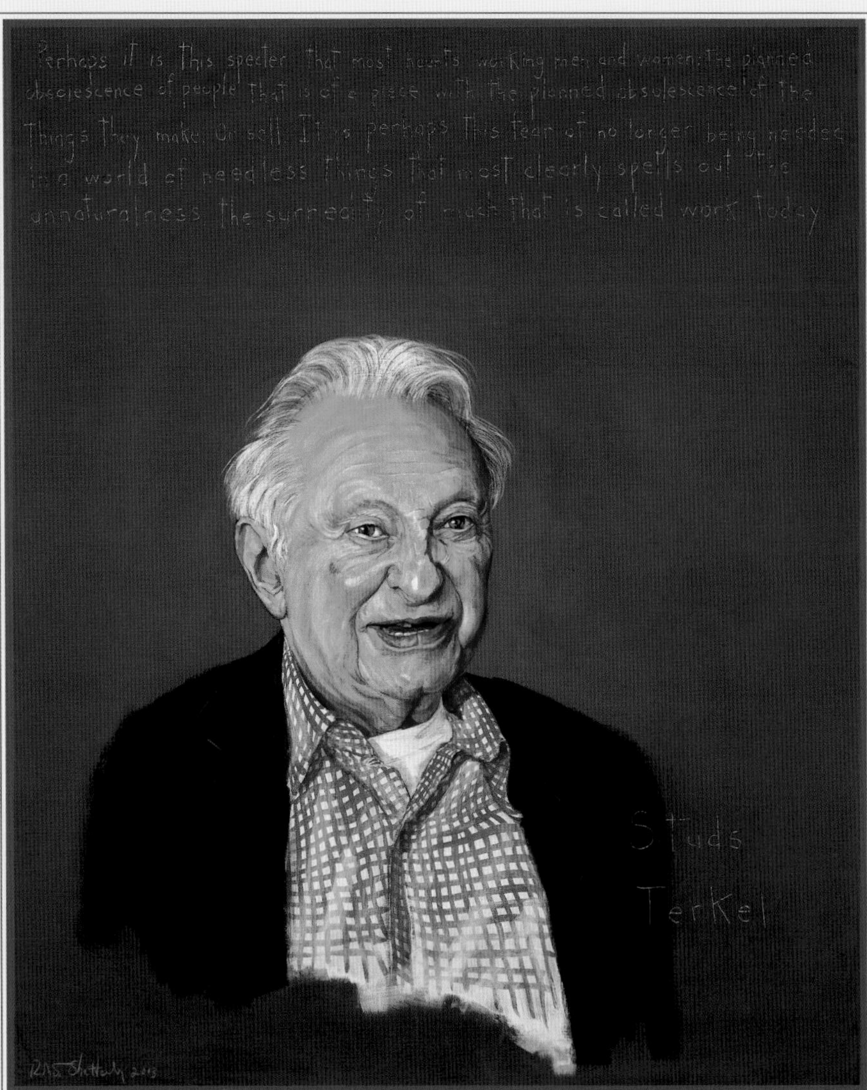

Perhaps it is this specter that most haunts working men and women: the planned obsolescence of people that is of a piece with the planned obsolescence of the things they make. Or sell. It is perhaps this fear of no longer being needed in a world of needless things that most clearly spells out the unnaturalness, the surreality of much that is called work today.

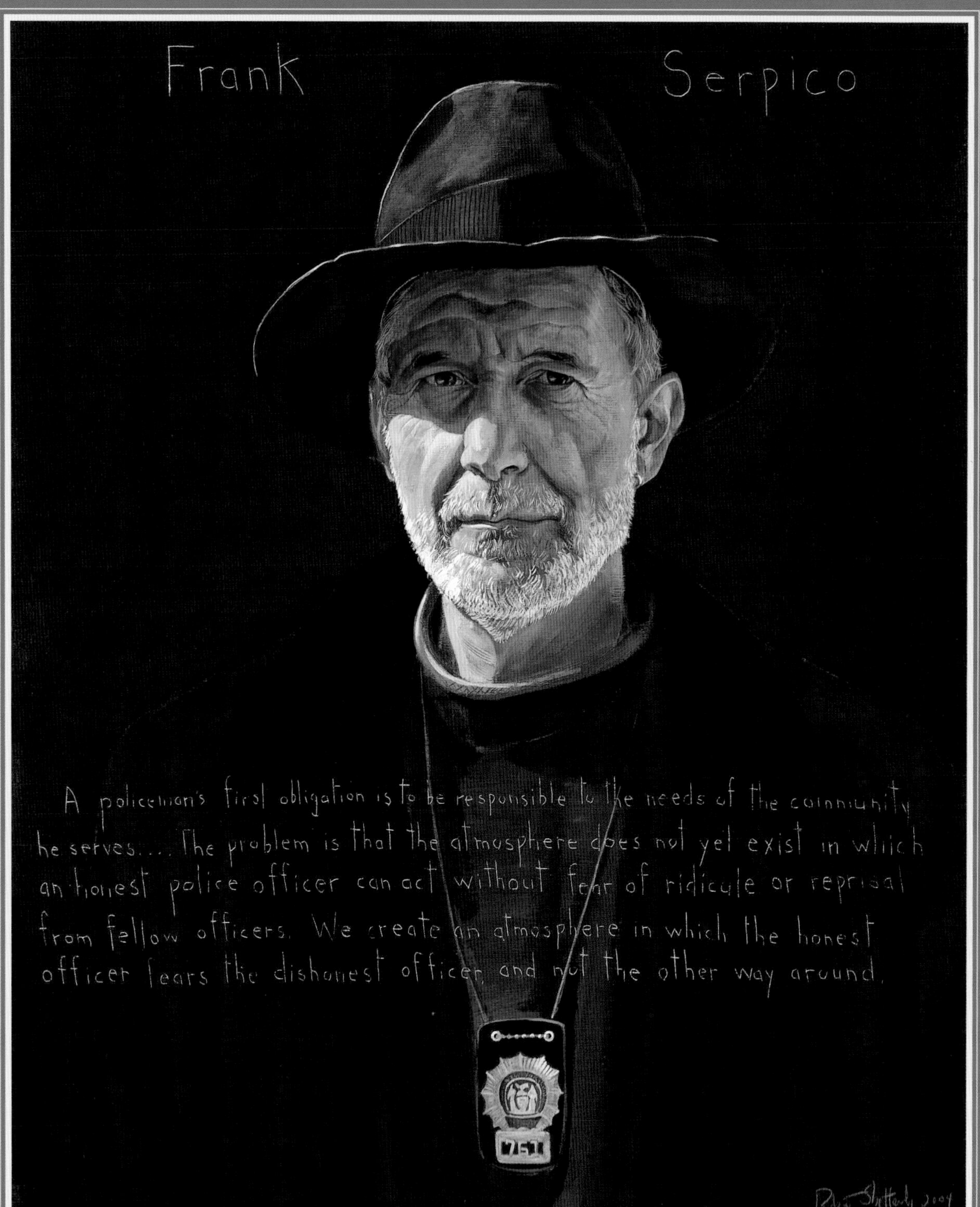
Frank Serpico
A policeman's first obligation is to be responsible to the needs of the community
he serves.... The problem is that the atmosphere does not yet exist in which
an honest police officer can act without fear of ridicule or reprisal
from fellow officers. We create an atmosphere in which the honest
officer fears the dishonest officer, and not the other way around.

Frank Serpico

Retired police detective, author, lecturer, 1936–

A policeman's first obligation is to be responsible to the needs of the community he serves...The problem is that the atmosphere does not yet exist in which an honest police officer can act without fear of ridicule or reprisal from fellow officers. We create an atmosphere in which the honest officer fears the dishonest officer, and not the other way around.

Jody Williams

Activist, writer, teacher, Nobel laureate, 1950–

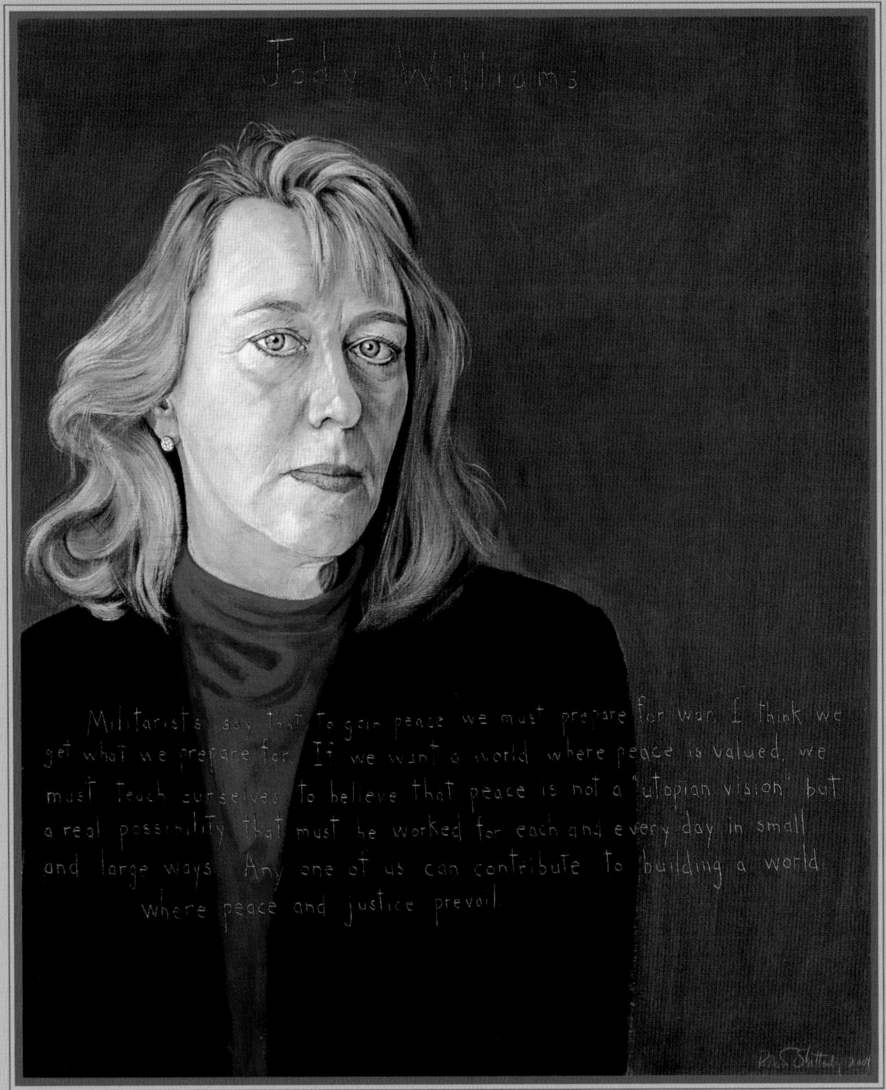

Militarists say that to gain peace we must prepare for war. I think we get what we prepare for. If we want a world where peace is valued, we must teach ourselves to believe that peace is not a "utopian vision" but a real responsibility that must be worked for each and every day in small and large ways. Any one of us can contribute to building a world where peace and justice prevail.

Amy Goodman

Journalist, host of Democracy Now!, *1957–*

I really do think that if for one week in the United States we saw the true face of war, we saw people's limbs sheared off, we saw kids blown apart, for one week, war would be eradicated. Instead, what we see in the U.S. media is the video war game. Our mission is to make dissent commonplace in America.

WILLIAM SLOANE COFFIN

Clergyman, social activist, 1924–

The war against Iraq is as disastrous as it is unnecessary; perhaps in terms of its wisdom, justice, purpose and motives, the worst war in American history. . . . Our military men and women . . . were not called to defend America but rather to attack Iraq. They were not called to die for, but rather to kill for, their country. What more unpatriotic thing could we have asked of our sons and daughters . . . ?

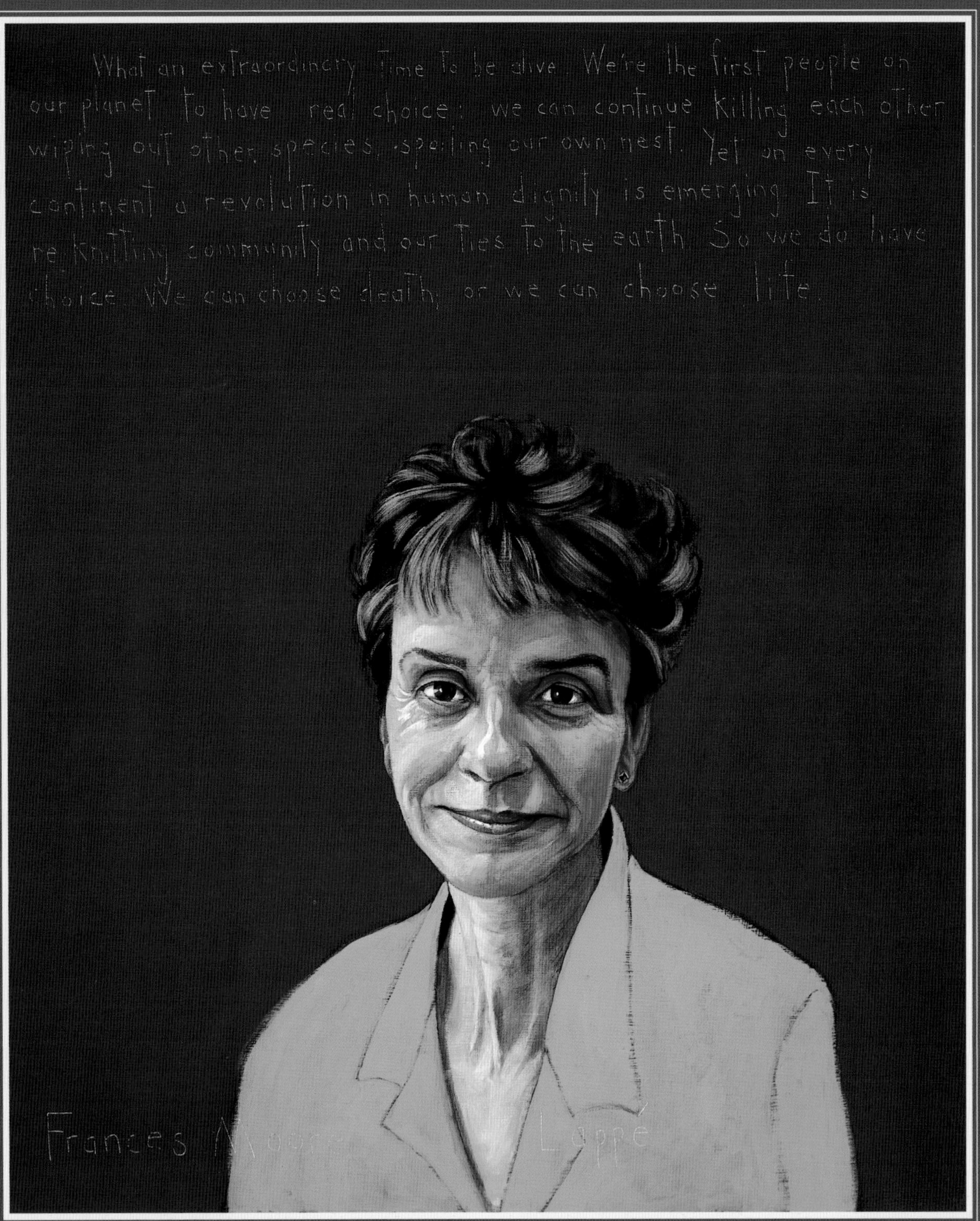

FRANCES MOORE LAPPÉ

Writer, activist, 1944–

What an extraordinary time to be alive. We're the first people on our planet to have real choice: we can continue killing each other, wiping out other species, spoiling our nest. Yet on every continent a revolution in human dignity is emerging. It is re-knitting community and our ties to the earth. So we do have a choice. We can choose death; or we can choose life.

Jane Addams • *1860–1935* • In 1889, Jane Addams and Ellen Gates Starr founded Hull-House in an impoverished section of Chicago, the first major settlement house in the United States. Hull-House provided a place for people who were down on their luck, out of work, sick, and homeless. Addams's work among the neighborhood people led her to publicly support labor unions and reform in labor laws.

Foreseeing the approach of World War I, Addams founded the Women's Peace Party and the International Congress of Women. She served as president of the Women's International League for Peace and Freedom from 1912 to 1929 and honorary president until her death. She was also a founder of the American Civil Liberties Union and the National Association for the Advancement of Colored People. In 1931, Jane Addams became the first American woman to be awarded the Nobel Peace Prize. *(p. 8)*

Muhammad Ali • *1942–* • When Muhammad Ali refused to fight in Vietnam because of his moral and political convictions, he was universally condemned. "I ain't got no quarrel with them Viet Cong," he said, adding, "No Viet Cong ever called me nigger." His courage isolated him. Labeled unpatriotic and cowardly, Ali was stripped of his heavyweight title and his boxing license. He was tried, found guilty, and sentenced to five years in prison. He was released on appeal, and three years later, the U.S. Supreme Court overturned the verdict. Muhammad Ali's courage to stand up for his beliefs set an example that was then followed by many other young men who agreed that the war in Vietnam was immoral. Now revered as an American icon, Ali was the first boxer to win the heavyweight championship three times. *(p. 23)*

Susan B. Anthony • *1820–1906* • Susan Brownell Anthony's dedication to social reform started early. She was born into the large family of a Quaker abolitionist. As a young teacher in western New York, Anthony addressed such thorny issues as equal pay for women teachers and broader educational opportunities for girls. Like other feminists of her time, she supported the temperance movement, which was attempting to stop the sale of alcohol. At a time when women were not allowed to divorce abusive men, she recognized in alcohol abuse the widespread suffering of women and children who had to endure the physical dangers and economic hardships of living with hard-drinking men.

In 1872, Anthony decided to test the protection of the Fourteenth Amendment, which said that all U.S. citizens have the rights to citizenship, but only men were allowed to vote. She attempted to register and vote in Rochester, New York, where she was arrested, tried, and fined, but she refused to pay. She said, "Trust me that as I ignore all law to help the slave, so will I ignore it all to protect the enslaved woman." *(p. 11)*

James Baldwin • *1924–1987* • James Baldwin, a great African-American writer, held a mirror up for Americans to see themselves more clearly. During the civil rights movement, he helped people everywhere understand better the nature and extent of racism. Born in Harlem and educated in New York City schools, James Baldwin gained literary prominence with the publication of his novels *Go Tell It on the Mountain* and *Giovanni's Room* and his essay collections *Notes of a Native Son, Nobody Knows My Name,* and *The Fire Next Time*.

Baldwin's insights were universally truthful: "People who treat other people as less than human must not be surprised when the bread that they have cast upon the waters comes back to them poisoned." *(p. 15)*

Wendell Berry • *1934–* • Wendell Berry, a farmer and writer in Kentucky, has been called the prophet of rural America. Simply put, Berry believes that humankind must learn to live in harmony with nature, or perish. The forces in our government and business world that want to grow the economy by exploiting natural resources and polluting the environment may be dooming the earth.

In his essay "The Failure of War" (1999), Berry asks: "How many deaths of other people's children are we willing to accept in order that we may be free, affluent, and (supposedly) at peace? To that question I answer: None . . . Don't kill any children for my benefit." *(p. 30)*

Rachel Carson • *1907–1964* • Rachel Carson is widely revered as the founder of the environmental movement in America. Her book *Silent Spring* (1962) was the first serious warning to the United States and the world that pesticides and pollution were causing terrible harm to the environment. Her carefully researched studies focused primarily on the pesticide DDT, which was banned in 1972. In 1992, a panel of distinguished Americans voted *Silent Spring* the most influential book of the past fifty years. However, pollution, use of harmful pesticides, loss of habitat, and overharvesting continue, despite the warning, and we are in the midst of a major extinction of plant and animal species caused by human mistreatment of the environment. *(p. 24)*

Cesar Chavez • *1927–1993* • At age ten, Chavez became a migrant farm worker, moving throughout the Southwest with his family. Frequently, there were no schools for the children, and the temporary housing was poor, wages low, hours long, working conditions dangerous because of the pesticides in the fields, and health care nonexistent. As an adult, Chavez returned to field work and decided to work toward bettering the lives of farm workers.

In 1962, Chavez founded the National Farm Workers' Association (NFWA). Ultimately, the NFWA became the United Farm Workers (UFW). Committed to nonviolence, Chavez's UFW organized extremely successful boycotts, and he personally put his life on the line by holding fasts to gain national attention. Because of Chavez's extraordinary efforts, farm workers gained higher pay, family health coverage, pension benefits, and respect. In 1991, he received the Águila Azteca (Aztec Eagle), and in 1994, he was posthumously presented with the Presidential Medal of Freedom. Chavez said, "We are poor. Our allies are few. But we have something the rich do not own. We have our own bodies and spirits and the justice of our cause as our weapons." *(p. 15)*

Chief Joseph • *c. 1840–1904* • Son of a Nez Percé Indian Chief, Joseph was born Hinmaton Yalaktit ("Thunder Rolling Down the Mountain") in what is now northeastern Oregon. When the political and military leaders of the United States forced his people from their native lands, Chief Joseph led a brilliant tactical retreat from the U.S. Cavalry across several states in the West. With this famous retreat, he was trying to escape with his tribe into Canada to avoid being forced onto a reservation. When he surrendered, Chief Joseph was told that his people would be returned to their lands in Oregon, but instead they were transported to eastern Kansas, and then to Oklahoma, where many died from epidemic diseases. He continued to protest their treatment, even traveling to Washington, D.C., in 1879 to meet with President Rutherford B. Hayes, but he and his people were never permitted to return to their homeland. He died in northeastern Washington State in 1904 and was buried there in exile. *(p. 8)*

Noam Chomsky • *1928–* • Noam Chomsky believes that when a government appeals to the prejudices and fears of people rather than their ability to be tolerant, that government can enlist people to act against their own best interests. That is, out of fear people may vote to spend their tax money on militarism and weapons when there is no real threat, rather than on education, health care, and environmental protection. As a historian, Chomsky points to many instances of fear and prejudice being used in this manner. Chomsky is well known as one of the world's foremost scholars of linguistics, but outside the university world, he is better known as a political activist—a role that he vigorously assumed as an early and outspoken critic and protestor of the Vietnam War. "I'm a citizen of the United States," says Chomsky, "and I have a share of responsibility for what it does. I'd like to see it act in ways that meet decent moral standards." *(p. 23)*

William Sloane Coffin • *1924–* • For more than forty years, the Reverend William Sloane Coffin has confronted major questions of morality and justice—civil rights, the Vietnam War, nuclear weapons, the Iraq war, environmental degradation, social inequality, and women's and gay rights—with courage and vision. His leadership has inspired many others to act with courage, too. He believes that "attacking worldwide poverty may be our best defense policy. It certainly would marginalize extremists and slow down the recruitment of new terrorists."

Coffin's commitment to humanity springs from his religious faith, and he asserts that faith requires political action: "To show compassion for an individual without showing concern for the structures of society that make him an object of compassion is to be sentimental rather than loving." And he says, " . . . if you lessen your anger at the structures of power, you lower your love for the victims of power." *(p. 35)*

Dorothy Day • *1897–1980* • Dorothy Day combined her passion for justice and equality with her religious commitment for serving the destitute. Concerned for the sufferings of the poor from a young age, she converted to Catholicism after the birth of her daughter and, feeling called by the Gospel to care for the hungry and despised, committed herself to a "revolution of the heart."

In Father Peter Maurin, Dorothy Day met a like-minded believer and reformer. In 1933, the two began the Catholic Worker Movement, which not only published an influential newspaper but founded a number of "hospitality houses" to serve the homeless. She took a vow of poverty and lived a life of service to the poor, working tirelessly for women's rights, workers' rights, and peace. *(p. 9)*

Frederick Douglass • *1818–1895* • Frederick Douglass was born into slavery. His love of learning flourished after a sympathetic slave owner's wife taught him to read, which was illegal. Nevertheless, Douglass read voraciously, and his impressive knowledge intimidated his owner, who hired him out to a cruel master in an effort to break his spirit. Douglass defied him in an act of great moral and physical courage and escaped to New York, where he began his career as an abolitionist orator, writer, newspaper publisher, and government official.

Douglass published three autobiographical books, the first of which was the most influential: *Narrative of the Life of Frederick Douglass, an American Slave, Written by Himself* (1845). He was also an early champion of women's rights. He said, "Power concedes nothing without a demand. It never did and it never will." *(p. 7)*

W.E.B. Du Bois • *1868–1963* • W.E.B. Du Bois was one of the first to recognize that poverty and race inequality were America's two major challenges of the twentieth century. He said: "To be a poor man is hard, but to be a poor race in a land of dollars is the very bottom of hardships."

A great thinker and a prolific writer, Du Bois brought intelligence, scholarly integrity, and moral purpose to his lifelong work for racial understanding and equality for all races. A list of his writings covers forty-five pages, but it is *The Souls of Black Folk* (1903), a collection of essays, sketches, and musical passages, that established him as one of the preeminent voices in the twentieth-century movement for justice and equality. Du Bois said, "One ever feels his twoness,—an American, a Negro; two souls, two thoughts, two unreconciled strivings; two warring ideals in one dark body, whose dogged strength alone keeps it from being torn asunder." *(p. 9)*

Marian Wright Edelman • *1939–* • Through the Children's Defense Fund, which she founded in 1973, Marian Wright Edelman has been advocating for the health, safety, and education needs of the children in the United States for over thirty years. The daughter of a Baptist minister, Mrs. Edelman earned her law degree from Yale and was the first black woman to be admitted to the Mississippi Bar. She directed the NAACP Legal Defense Educational Fund office in Jackson, Mississippi, before moving to Washington, D.C., to serve as counsel for the Poor People's Campaign organized by Dr. Martin Luther King, Jr. As founder, leader, and principal spokesperson for the Children's Defense Fund, Mrs. Edelman has worked to persuade Congress to overhaul foster care, support adoption, improve child care, and protect children who are handicapped, homeless, abused, or neglected. A philosophy of service absorbed during her childhood underlies all her efforts. She is a voice for the voiceless. As she expresses it, "If you don't like the way the world is, you have an obligation to change it. Just do it one step at a time." *(p. 3)*

Dwight Eisenhower • *1890–1969* • "Ike," as Eisenhower was widely known, is remembered today as the Allied commander who planned and executed the D-day invasion of France during World War II. That invasion ultimately led to the liberation of Europe from Nazi domination. In 1949–1950, he reentered civilian life, and in 1950, President Truman appointed him supreme commander of the North Atlantic Treaty Organization (NATO).

Dwight Eisenhower's great popularity won him the Republican nomination in 1952; he was elected president when the country was mired in the Korean War. He kept his campaign promise to end that conflict in 1953. He said, "The cost of one modern heavy bomber is this: a modern brick school in more than 30 cities. It is two electric power plants, each serving a town of 60,000 people. It is two fine, fully equipped hospitals." *(p. 20)*

Emma Goldman • *1869–1940* • Emma Goldman was born in Kovno, Russia, and emigrated to the United States when she was fifteen. Her family's financial hardships forced her to leave school and work in a sweatshop, where she quickly identified with the concerns of poor workers and became a political activist.

In her writing and public speaking, Emma Goldman championed free speech, birth control, women's rights, racial equality, and labor unions. She was arrested and detained several times for her activism, but her most severe punishment, two years in prison, was for obstructing the draft during World War I. She believed the United States did not need to fight in the war, that it was not a war for democracy but for business. In 1919, she was deported to Russia, where she witnessed the consequences of the 1917 revolution. Disillusioned by the Communist dictatorship, she left the Soviet Union in 1921, and spent the rest of her life fighting for the rights of those displaced by war and speaking out against fascism. Goldman said, "Resistance to tyranny is man's highest ideal." *(p. 17)*

Amy Goodman • *1957–* • Amy Goodman is the host of *Democracy Now!,* an independent news program broadcast by Pacifica Radio, the only source of independent news in the United States that takes no corporate money. *Democracy Now!* is broadcast five days a week on over 225 radio and television stations across North America. Every day Goodman presents a range of opinions not often heard on the airwaves. She believes that mainstream media are so compromised by political influence and corporate money that they no longer tell people the truth. She says, "A democratic media gives us hope. . . . When people hear their neighbors given a voice, see their struggles in what they watch and read, spirits are lifted. People feel like they can make a difference." *(p. 34)*

Woody Guthrie • *1912–1967* • Woodrow Wilson Guthrie wrote over a thousand songs, including such classics as "This Land Is Your Land," "So Long (It's Been Good to Know Yuh)," and "Deportee." Perhaps because he grew up during the Great Depression, a hard time for both his family and his country, Woody hated "a song that makes you think that you're not any good." He often traveled to where people were facing difficult times and wrote songs about their experiences to make them feel better.

His many cross-country trips opened his eyes to a land where people went hungry, and the lives and health of immigrants and union workers were threatened by moneyed interests. When he sang about such things, some called him a populist; others, a Socialist or Communist. "Left wing, right wing, chicken wing—it's all the same to me," Woody replied. "I sing my songs wherever I can sing 'em." *(p. 19)*

Doris Haddock ("Granny D") • *1910–* • Doris Haddock reminds us that our country is made up of individuals, each with an important responsibility. "We must not be content to go home and watch television when there is a democracy to run, or to spend all our money on ourselves and our children. . . . Get involved in community issues. . . . That is the life of free people in a democracy."

"Granny D" is best known today for her walk across America in support of campaign-finance reform. Passionate about the need to remove the influence of special interest money from the democratic process, she spoke to countless Americans on a trip that lasted fourteen months, covered 3,200 miles, and wore out four pairs of shoes.

Commitment to campaign-finance reform is one facet of her activist career that spans working on environmental issues in Alaska, writing and speaking against the war in Iraq, and running for U.S. senator from New Hampshire at the age of ninety-four. She says, "If we lose control of our government, then we lose our ability to dispense justice and human kindness." *(p. 28)*

Jim Hightower • *1943–* • Jim Hightower is a journalist whose mission is to reveal the truth, and he uses humor to get people thinking and acting. To him, *agitator* is not a negative word. "Being an agitator is what America is all about," Hightower says. "If it was not for the agitators of circa 1776, we'd all still be singing 'God Save the Queen.'" An agitator, he adds, "is the center post in the washing machine that gets the dirt out." It is the pressure of conformity that keeps people from having the courage to want to think independently, find out the truth, and be responsible for that truth.

Hightower operates as a modern-day Johnny Appleseed, constantly on the road visiting America's grass roots. He publishes a monthly newsletter, broadcasts daily radio commentaries, has hosted his own talk-radio show, and travels with his Rolling Thunder Chautauqua Tours, a combination of country-fair fun and popular activism. *(p. 27)*

Zora Neale Hurston • *1891–1960* • Born and reared in an all-black, self-governed town in central Florida, Zora Neale Hurston absorbed the rich history of centuries-old folktales and a distinctive Southern black culture. As an important part of the Harlem Renaissance (1920–1940), Hurston has been called the "foremother" of a generation of black American women writers. Zora Neale Hurston published three novels, including *Their Eyes Were Watching God,* three books of folklore, short stories, an autobiography, a one-act play, and several librettos; nonetheless, she died, largely forgotten, in degrading poverty. Today her depiction of black American culture is fully appreciated, and her writing and influence have been restored to their rightful place in American letters. She said, "Grab the broom of anger and drive off the beast of fear." *(p. 20)*

Molly Ivins • *1944–* • Journalist Molly Ivins stands out in her profession not only for her courage to write and speak the truth, but for her use of humor to lampoon the self-seeking, the corrupt, and the incompetent. Her wit and insight place her squarely in the tradition of American's great political humorists like Mark Twain. Ivins began her newspaper career with the *Houston Chronicle* and then moved to the *Minneapolis Tribune,* where she became the city's first female police reporter. Returning to her home state as coeditor of the *Texas Observer,* she concentrated on politics and social justice issues. In 1976, Ivins became a political reporter for the *New York Times*. After working as a columnist for other papers, Molly Ivins became an independent journalist. Comments like this have made her well known for her forthrightness and humor: "Drag God into politics, and you'll ruin His reputation in no time." *(p. 27)*

Mary Harris "Mother" Jones • *1830–1930* • Mother Jones was a great labor organizer in support of mine workers and against child labor during the late nineteenth century and early twentieth century. At that time, the United States government, courts, and police frequently worked together to protect mine owners from having to pay the miners living wages and provide healthy working conditions. Only by organizing unions could the workers win their rights.

Mother Jones was a tiny woman with incredible courage and great speaking ability who dedicated her life to protecting poor people and their children from exploitation. She worked tirelessly to advance social and political causes, such as the abolition of child labor, and to organize the United Mine Workers. In 1905, she helped found the International Workers of the World (IWW). She often said, "Pray for the dead and fight like hell for the living!" *(p. 14)*

HELEN KELLER • *1880–1968* • Helen Keller is remembered primarily for her incredible triumph over deafness and blindness to become one of the most prominent people of the late nineteenth and twentieth centuries. She traveled the world with her teacher and interpreter, Anne Sullivan, showing that with the proper instruction, the disabled could become productive members of society and lead much fuller lives. She was not solely concerned with the welfare of the disabled. She taught that all people were incapacitated when they didn't become active citizens in defense of their own interests, rights, and freedoms. She strongly supported such groups as the Socialist Party, the American Civil Liberties Union, the International Workers of the World, and the National Association for the Advancement of Colored People, and campaigned for birth control, civil rights, women's suffrage, and world peace. *(p. 26)*

KATHY KELLY • *1953–* • Kathy Kelly has been nominated for the Nobel Peace Prize three times since 2000. In 1996, she helped to found Voices in the Wilderness, a group that brought attention to the suffering caused by the sanctions imposed on Iraq by the U. S. and the United Nations. When many people think of the goal of war, they don't see the innocent people who get caught in war. More than 500,000 Iraqi children died from malnutrition and lack of medicine while the sanctions were in place during the 1990s. Kathy Kelly and Voices in the Wilderness took medical supplies and toys to the children. When the Bush administration declared war on Iraq in 2003, Kelly stayed in Baghdad to help where she could. Kelly traces her activism to her childhood. In high school she began to read about the Holocaust. "I remember thinking that I never, ever, ever, ever want to be the person who is trying to be an innocent bystander while something that awful goes on." *(p. 22)*

MARTIN LUTHER KING, JR. • *1929–1968* • Martin Luther King, Jr. was one of America's greatest civil rights leaders and peace activists. His campaigns for racial equality were nonviolent because he believed that violence leads to a cycle of anger, fear, and revenge, while nonviolence and civil disobedience appeal to people's consciences and allow for reconciliation.

Dr. King studied the writings and example of Mahatma Gandhi in India, who powerfully influenced his philosophy of nonviolence. When he accepted the Nobel Peace Prize in 1964, Dr. King said: "Nonviolence is not sterile passivity, but a powerful moral force which makes for social transformation."

As a leader of many demonstrations in support of rights of African-Americans, Dr. King was subject to frequent arrest, imprisonment, and threats. He was assassinated on April 4, 1968, in Memphis, Tennessee, while supporting a sanitation workers' strike. In 1999, a Memphis jury concluded that King's assassination had not been the work of a lone gunman but a conspiracy of underworld, police, and government forces. *(p. 13)*

JONATHAN KOZOL • *1936–* • For the past forty years, Jonathan Kozol has been trying to get the United States to pay attention to the fact that public education is failing its students who are growing up in poverty. Poor children in inner cities all across the country go to overcrowded, dilapidated schools in dangerous neighborhoods. Much less is spent on them per pupil than in schools of middle- and upper-class communities. Their lives are so hard and the education so bad that most kids drop out. The whole point of education is to give all children the opportunity to achieve, to live out their dreams, and to participate in a democratic society. In his hard-hitting books, Jonathan Kozol asks, Is this the America we want? *(p. 29)*

DOROTHEA LANGE • *1895–1965* • Dorothea Lange believed that the camera could teach people "how to see without a camera." She is most famous for her photographs of refuges fleeing the Dust Bowl during the Great Depression of the 1930s. Her work reflects insight, compassion, and profound empathy for her subjects. By documenting the sufferings of the out-of-work migrants, she believed she could help people to see a reality they couldn't imagine from words alone. In fact, when her photograph "Migrant Mother" was published, hundreds of people sent the workers food, clothing, money, and blankets. She also photographed the people and conditions in the Japanese internment camps during World War II. That experience caused her to make the statement quoted on her portrait. *(p. 21)*

Lewis Lapham • *1935–* • Since 1983 Lewis Lapham has been the editor of *Harpers* magazine, in which he writes a monthly essay about American politics and culture. His essays attack hypocrisy in our government, business, and personal practices and values. Just before the U.S. attack on Iraq in 2003, Lapham said, "War is easier than peace. The government elects to punish an enemy it perceives as weak because it is easier to send an aircraft carrier to the Persian Gulf than to attempt the harder task of making American society not so wretchedly defaced by its hungry children, its crowded prisons, and its corporate thieves. . . ." Lapham was awarded the National Magazine Award in 1995 for expressing an "exhilarating point of view in an age of conformity." *(p. 31)*

Frances Moore Lappé • *1944–* • Frances Moore Lappé's work demonstrates that there can be enough food to feed the hungry, and we can serve the needs of community and business at the same time. She was a "twenty-six-year-old trusting her common sense" when she began the research that led to the publication of *Diet for a Small Planet,* a book that sold over three million copies and changed the way people think about food. Her book showed that food scarcity results when grain, rich in nutrients and capable of supporting vast populations, is fed to livestock to produce meat, which yields only a fraction of those nutrients. For instance, sixteen pounds of grain and soy protein need to be fed to a steer to produce one pound of meat protein. If more people got their protein from grains, there would be plenty to go around. Today she is focusing her attention on communities of people around the world who, when their governments have failed to address their needs, have democratically organized themselves to protect their cultures and advance themselves economically and politically. *(p. 36)*

Perry Mann • *1921–* • Perry Mann is a columnist for the *Nicholas Chronicle* of Summersville, West Virginia. He writes deeply on wide-ranging issues, including politics, ecology, history, economics, civil rights, religion, philosophy, and rural life. Working and living with nature have taught him to respect the great web of life, which he believes is much stronger than any human activity. By abusing the earth and not realizing that we need to support the health of this web, he believes we are in danger of destroying ourselves and much of the earth's life forms with us. Not well known outside of his community in West Virginia, Perry Mann represents the importance of thousands of unheralded and critically important voices across our country. *(p. 31)*

John Muir • *1838–1914* • From the late 1800s until his death in 1914, John Muir was the most important conservationist in the United States. His relationship to the land and all of its creatures was spiritual. He said, "No synonym for God is so perfect as Beauty. Whether as seen carving the lines of mountains with glaciers, or gathering matter into stars, or planning the movements of water, or gardening—still all is Beauty!" Because of his intense relationship with nature's beauty, he wanted to preserve as much of it as possible. In 1892, he and his supporters founded the Sierra Club, of which he served as president for the rest of his life, "to do something for wilderness." Muir convinced President Theodore Roosevelt that America's beautiful wilderness areas were worth saving, and so Yosemite, Sequoia, Mount Rainier, Petrified Forest, and Grand Canyon National Parks were created. *(p. 6)*

Ralph Nader • *1934–* • For the past fifty years, Ralph Nader has worked to keep our products safe and our government honest. He became famous in 1965 when he published a report on the American automobile industry, which led to a series of congressional investigations and tighter regulations for safer cars. Since 1966, Nader has worked to pass at least eight major consumer protection laws, including the Safe Drinking Water Act and the founding of such agencies as the Occupational Safety and Health Administration (OSHA), the Environmental Protection Agency (EPA), and the Consumer Product Safety Administration. He has promoted better access to government with the Freedom of Information Act, and he has founded many organizations to carry out his wide-ranging research and advocacy. *(p. 26)*

Rosa Parks • *1913–* • On December 1, 1955, in Montgomery, Alabama, Rosa Parks was riding home from work on a city bus. The bus driver asked her to give up her seat to a white man and to move to the back of the bus. She refused, and for this courageous act of civil disobedience, she was arrested, fingerprinted, and put in jail. The Montgomery bus boycott, led by Martin Luther King, Jr., began that night and lasted 382 days. It was so successful in causing financial hardship to the city bus company that Montgomery agreed to integrate the buses. In 1956, the U.S. Supreme Court declared that segregation of public transportation is against the law. *(p. 12)*

Paul Robeson • *1898–1976* • There was a time in the 1940s when, it may be safe to say, Paul Robeson, a man of extraordinary talent in whatever he chose to do, was the best-known African-American in the world. He traveled the world, singing songs to people in their own languages. Traveling and performing abroad gave him the chance to learn that "the essential character of a nation is determined . . . by the common people, and that the common people of all nations are truly brothers in the great family of mankind." People everywhere loved him. When he returned to the United States, Robeson became an outspoken critic of racism. He refused to sing before segregated audiences and led an antilynching campaign. To punish him for his outspoken honesty about racism, the United States government took away his passport, never charging him with a crime. He was blacklisted as a performer and was unable to make a good living. In effect, he was silenced. Shortly before his death, he wrote his autobiography, *Here I Stand*, in which he said, "The artist must elect to fight for Freedom or for Slavery. I have made my choice. I had no alternative." *(p. 19)*

Eleanor Roosevelt • *1884–1962* • Eleanor Roosevelt was born to privilege but her sympathies were with the less fortunate. From an early age she understood that "Without equality there can be no democracy." Her marriage in 1905 to Franklin Roosevelt, a distant cousin, brought her a large family to raise and, in 1921, a disabled husband to care for. With her encouragement, her husband became governor of New York and, in 1933, president.

As first lady, Eleanor Roosevelt knew that in a society divided by wealth and opportunity, people who are disadvantaged often are made to feel inferior. She used her position of prominence to promote better housing, more humane working conditions, and racial justice. She wrote a daily newspaper column, spoke on the radio, and traveled the country to observe and report on the plight of the forgotten poor. During World War II, she made many trips overseas and, at war's end and after the death of her husband, she was made a delegate to the United Nations. In 1946, she became chairman of the Commission on Human Rights. She asked, "When will our consciences grow so tender that we will act to prevent human misery rather than avenge it?" *(p. 18)*

Frank Serpico • *1936–* • Frank Serpico always wanted to be a police officer. He wanted to serve his community by helping people be safer. He was shocked to find, from his very first day on the job, that many of the policemen he was working with were taking bribes. They were agreeing not to arrest criminals involved in gambling, drug dealing, and prostitution in exchange for money. He was even more shocked to find that when he told the police chiefs about what he discovered, they did nothing. He suspected that the chiefs were themselves taking bribes. Even though his life was threatened, he told the *New York Times*. Only then, when the story went public, did things start to change. Serpico resigned from the NYPD after he was shot in a drug raid. He continues to speak out against the weakening of civil liberties and corrupt practices in law enforcement. *(p. 33)*

Margaret Chase Smith • *1897–1995* • Unable to afford a college education, Margaret Chase Smith held jobs as a teacher, telephone operator, newspaper circulation manager, and executive at a textile mill. In 1936, when her husband, Clyde, was elected to the U.S. House of Representatives, she accompanied him to Washington as his assistant.

Four years later. she was a widow, completing her husband's term in office. Elected to Congress in her own right, she served four terms in the House before being elected to the U.S. Senate. During this time, Senator Joseph McCarthy began to incite fear of Communism in the United States and used that fear to destroy the reputations and livelihoods of many Americans with leftist political beliefs. Smith was the first senator with the courage to denounce Senator McCarthy, and she was the only woman in the Senate at that time. Smith was the first woman to serve in both houses of Congress, the first to be elected to the Senate, and the first to have her name placed in nomination for the presidency at a national party convention. *(p. 18)*

Samantha Smith • *1972–1985* • From about 1950 to 1989, the United States and the Soviet Union (Russia) were entrenched in a cold war. Neither side fired a shot; instead, both sides built more and more nuclear weapons in response to the perceived threat from the other. Hundreds of millions of people lived in fear that either by aggression or accident, a war would start and the whole world would be destroyed.

In 1982, Samantha Smith, then ten years old, wrote a letter to Yuri Andropov, the premier of the Soviet Union. She wanted to know if the Soviet Union intended to start a war. Premier Andropov wrote her back, inviting her to come to the Soviet Union to judge for herself.

Samantha's trip to the Soviet Union was a great success. She believed the Soviets had no desire to start a war, and the trip so inspired her that she became an international spokesperson for peace.

Tragically, at the age of thirteen, Samantha and her father were killed in a plane crash when returning to Maine from a television appearance. *(p. 3)*

Elizabeth Cady Stanton • *1815–1902* • Elizabeth Cady Stanton worked with Susan B. Anthony for fifty years to try to win the vote for women. Stanton was a gifted writer and speaker, Anthony a dynamic organizer. It wasn't until 1920, after both had died, that American women finally got the vote. Susan B. Anthony believed that when women got the vote, all other forms of discrimination against women would fall away. Elizabeth Cady Stanton thought that this discrimination was much more institutionalized, that for women to be fully equal, major changes would have to take place in the workplace, the churches, marriage and divorce laws, property ownership, dress codes, education, and government. She was right. Neither shied away from their uphill battle, though. In spite of harassment, opposition, and threats, they steadfastly advocated for women's rights. *(p.10)*

Louis "Studs" Terkel • *1912–* • Studs Terkel is most famous as host of a series of radio and television shows in Chicago, starting in 1944. He has made it his mission for sixty years to find and report the ideas and feelings of people from every class, gender, and ethnic background. His television career was disrupted when he was blacklisted in 1953 for speaking out in favor of price and rent controls, against the poll tax and Jim Crow laws, and for refusing to cooperate with the House Un-American Activities Committee. He continued on the radio with a daily music and interview show, *The Studs Terkel Program,* which ran from 1952 to 1997. Studs likes to call himself "a guerilla journalist with a tape recorder." *(p. 32)*

Henry David Thoreau • *1817–1862* • Henry David Thoreau began the most famous experiment in solitary living in American history in 1845, when he moved to Walden Pond and built a small cabin. He transformed the notes and journal entries he kept during that time into the timeless text of *Walden,* an account of how one may achieve understanding of one's true nature by simplifying life and observing nature closely.

For over 150 years, Thoreau's observations and writings have influenced the thinking of millions, including Mahatma Gandhi and Martin Luther King, Jr.. He believed in the power of the individual citizen and stressed the individual's responsibility to stop abuses in our government. *(p. 5)*

Sojourner Truth • *1797–1883* • Sojourner Truth was born a slave in New York in 1797. In addition to all the horrible treatment she endured, she also saw her husband and five children sold away from her. In 1827, she escaped, and two years later New York State freed its slaves. While working as a servant, she heard a voice that she took to be the voice of God instructing her to take the name of Sojourner Truth and "to travel up and down the land, showing the people their sins and being a sign to them." She spent the rest of her long life doing just that, speaking out against the Constitution that promised justice but legalized slavery and denied women, African-Americans, and Native Americans their civil rights.

A charismatic speaker with a commanding presence, Sojourner never used notes for her speeches, for she never learned to read or write. Her speeches and autobiography were written down by her neighbor Frances Gage. *(p. 4)*

Mark Twain • *1835–1910* • Mark Twain was born Samuel Langhorne Clemens. His pseudonym is a riverboat leadsman's call; *mark twain* means that the boat is in a safe two fathoms of water. It is an ironic pen name for a man whose life seldom sailed smooth water.

Mark Twain is perhaps best known as the author of *The Adventures of Huckleberry Finn*. Before he was an established writer, he was a printer, steamboat pilot, Confederate soldier in constant retreat, silver miner, journalist, and lecturer. Throughout his life he championed the underdog, lampooned the powerful, and boosted humane causes. He hated slavery, war, hypocrisy, and politicians who pretended to represent all the people but worked primarily to advance the interests of the rich. He also knew that people would listen to him if he could make them laugh while he told the truth. Legislative bodies were a frequent target of his satiric wit: "I think I can say, and say with pride, that we have some legislatures that bring higher prices than any in the world." *(p. 6)*

Ida B. Wells • *1862–1931* • When Ida B. Wells was twenty-two, she defied a conductor's order to move to a segregated railroad car and was forcibly removed. She won a lawsuit against the railroad and, from that point on, worked consistently to overcome injustices to people of color and to women. In 1889, she became co-owner of a Memphis newspaper, *Free Speech and Headlight*. Her editorial protesting the lynching of three black friends led to a boycott of white businesses, the destruction of her newspaper offices, and threats against her life. Undeterred, she moved to Chicago, where she spent much of her adult life trying to protect the rights of African-Americans and to stop lynching. She was the founder of the National Association for the Advancement of Colored People (NAACP) and established the Negro Fellowship League for black men. *(p. 12)*

WALT WHITMAN • *1819–1892* • Walt Whitman, a self-described "mate and companion of people, all just as immortal and fathomless as myself," worked at a variety of occupations: drifter, printer, teacher, reporter, editor, novelist, and nurse. The celebrated "melting pot" of New York City in the 1840s provided him an education in diversity and democratic values. When he was thirty-six, he published *Leaves of Grass,* consisting of twelve long, untitled poems, which he revised and expanded throughout his life. No subject was off-limits to Whitman. He celebrated the body and all its functions as exuberantly as he did the spirit. He also broke the formal restraints of poetry in his time by writing in unrhymed verse. Ralph Waldo Emerson acknowledged Whitman's new poetic voice as "the most wonderful gift . . . the most extraordinary piece of wit and wisdom that America has yet contributed." *(p. 2)*

JUDY WICKS • *1947–* • When Judy Wicks opened her restaurant, the White Dog Café, in Philadelphia, she set out to test her theory that a well-run business could pay its workers living wages, buy its resources from local businesses, be good to the environment, donate to social services, and make a profit. As a result, the White Dog Café invests in wind-generated power and buys seasonal produce from locally owned organic farms and meats from farms that raise animals humanely. Twenty percent of profits go to the White Dog Café Foundation and other nonprofits. Wicks has put in place more progressive business practices per square foot than any other entrepreneur in America. Now the recipient of many local and national awards, Wicks helped to found the Business Alliance for Local Living Economies (BALLE) to teach other businesspeople how to be better community and world citizens. *(p. 32)*

JODY WILLIAMS • *1950–* • In wartime, soldiers sometimes protect themselves from attack by planting land mines in the ground. When triggered, these small bombs sometimes kill a person outright. Most often, though, they inflict horrible wounds, blowing off a foot, leg, or arm. Usually, at the end of a war, no one removes the mines. Millions are still hidden in many parts of the world. Twenty thousand mines explode every year, injuring civilians.

Jody Williams wanted to change this. In 1992, she founded and coordinated the International Campaign to Ban Landmines. For five years she was its chief organizer and spokesperson, working with governments and organizations around the world. In 1997, the campaign achieved its goal: an international treaty banning antipersonnel land mines was put into effect. Jody Williams was awarded the Nobel Peace Prize for her work. She now teaches, writes, and lectures extensively. *(p. 34)*

TERRY TEMPEST WILLIAMS • *1955–* • Terry Tempest Williams has turned her lifelong love of the desert into a spiritual and political commitment to preserving the fragile red-rock wilderness of southern Utah. She asks, "Who can say how much nature can be destroyed without consequence? Who can say how much land can be used for extractive purposes until it is rendered barren forever? And who can say what the human spirit will be crying out for one hundred years from now?" She writes powerfully about these issues, and her books and essays have won her widespread admiration. Williams is the author of *Refuge* and, most recently, *The Open Space of Democracy*. She says, "We must all ask ourselves as Americans, 'Can we really survive the worship of our own destructiveness?'" *(p. 25)*

HOWARD ZINN • *1922–* • Howard Zinn is best known for his book *A People's History of the United States: 1942–Present,* a history of America through the perspective of "those outside of the political and economic establishment." Most history is written by people who have power, who are the conquerors. Their histories justify their actions. Zinn is an active advocate for the underclass, a proponent of world peace, and an articulate critic of corporate power and greed. "We need new ways of thinking," says Zinn. "We need to rethink our position in the world. We need to stop sending weapons to countries that oppress people. We need to decide that we will not go to war, whatever reason is conjured up by the politicians or the media, because war in our time is always indiscriminate, a war against innocents, a war against children." *(p. 16)*

This book of portraits is dedicated to all those who have fought with such persistence and courage to close the gap between what the United States says about equality, justice, and democracy and what it does. Justice is not guaranteed in our Constitution; it is guaranteed by the love we have for it in our hearts, the truths we are willing to tell, and the degree to which we are willing to struggle for it.

Acknowledgments

First, I have to thank my partner, Gail Page, for her love and support and her honest, critical eye that has helped to make each portrait better. Without the tireless, optimistic, organizing help of Bob Sargent, a new and trusted friend, these paintings would not have become a traveling show. Special thanks to Anne Cushman for volunteering so many hours to research and write biographies, and to Richard Sassaman, who also helped enormously with the writing and research. Paul Newlin, too. Thanks to Marcia Kola for all the time she volunteered in the planning and organizing. Many thanks to Ken Woisand for designing and maintaining the website. And to Jay York of Affordable Photo for donating his excellent services. Thanks to Kim Ridley, editor of *Hope* magazine, for her advice about and help with meeting many of the subjects, and to Mark Baldwin and Dee Knisley at Borealis Press for producing the cards. Thanks to my editor at Dutton, Maureen Sullivan, for her belief in this project and her concern for accuracy. It's been a pleasure to work with her. And to Irene Vandervoort for her superb book design. And thanks to my agent, Edite Kroll, for all of her good advice and support. Thanks especially to my loving children, Aran and Caitlin, for the inspiration of their own work and their help in finding venues for the portraits. And thanks to the many, many others who, with suggestions and encouragement, financial and moral, kept me going. And, of course, on behalf of the people of the United States of present, past, and future generations, I thank all those who have dedicated and sacrificed so much to tell the truth. The consent of the governed, democracy, is meaningless unless the people know the truth. Unless we admit what we do, we can't know who we are.

✦ *For curriculum support and information about the traveling art show, visit www.americanswhotellthetruth.org* ✦

+ *Jane Addams*
+ *Muhammad Ali*
+ *Susan B. Anthony*
+ *James Baldwin*
+ *Wendell Berry*
+ *Rachel Carson*
+ *Cesar Chavez*
+ *Chief Joseph*
+ *Noam Chomsky*
+ *William Sloane Coffin*
+ *Dorothy Day*
+ *Frederick Douglass*
+ *W.E.B. Du Bois*
+ *Marian Wright Edelman*
+ *Dwight Eisenhower*
+ *Emma Goldman*
+ *Amy Goodman*
+ *Woody Guthrie*
+ *Doris Haddock ("Granny D")*
+ *Jim Hightower*
+ *Zora Neale Hurston*
+ *Molly Ivins*
+ *Mary Harris "Mother" Jones*
+ *Helen Keller*
+ *Kathy Kelly*
+ *Martin Luther King, Jr.*